D0688950

good for you

Dana Jacobi

PHOTOGRAPHS
Erin Kunkel

weldon**owen**

start with the plant

The way I like to eat is easy and intuitive. Put simply, it means focusing on plant-based meals that are delicious and creative as well as wholesome. The foundation for the recipes in this book is a Mediterranean-style diet emphasizing fruits and vegetables, whole grains, and legumes. Some recipes add poultry, fish, or meat for heartiness and additional protein. I also believe in using healthy fats, flavorful and low-fat dairy foods, plus herbs and spices to give dishes bold flavors. I love using nuts and seeds to enhance dishes.

The recipes in this book feature short ingredient lists and sensible prep times. In some dishes, a combination may be unexpected or it gives a simple ethnic twist to healthful ingredients, as in Sicilian-Style Shrimp with Cauliflower and Almonds, North African–Style Bulgur and Grilled Vegetable Salad, and Indian Spiced Roasted Beets. Other recipes make healthy versions of favorites such as Three-Berry Cobbler, and Huevos Rancheros.

Sharing good times is also part of well-being, so this is food that brings people together with pleasure. For me, this is as important as eating less meat and using ingredients rich in antioxidants. Good eating also means enjoying variety—a bit of everything in moderation—rather than following strict rules for what you should eat and what to avoid.

What is good for you can also be good for the planet and your community, so I support buying from local farmers and producers, including those who treat livestock humanely. I point out where organic produce may be desirable and share recommendations from the Environmental Defense Fund. All the seafood choices meet sustainability standards used by Monterey Bay Aquarium's Seafood Watch.

I hope that this book ends up a dog-eared kitchen companion, a source of helpful, health-supporting information, and that its dishes become favorites that your family and friends look forward to sharing.

Dana Jacobi

cabbages & crucifers

Brassicas are loaded with vitamins C, A, beta-carotene, and minerals. Sulfur compounds that neutralize carcinogens contribute to their strong taste. Eating just an ounce a day of crucifers can significantly lower cancer risk.

BROCCOLI

Broccoli contains potent substances that help your body neutralize and get rid of cancer-causing toxins. Most of its goodness is in the florets, especially those with a bluish or purple cast. Whirl in some florets while making pesto for a nutrient boost.

BOK CHOY

Loaded with calcium and potassium as well as vitamin A and beta-carotene, this mild-flavored Asian cabbage is good thinly sliced and added raw to salads as well as stir-fried. Separate the creamy, crisp stems to cook first, then add the dark green leaves. Baby bok choy is lower in nutrients.

for more on broccoli/ broccolini see page 146

BRUSSELS SPROUTS

You get 4 grams of protein, along with vitamins A, C, and folate, plus a generous amount of carotenoids in one cup of cooked brussels sprouts. So they cook evenly, select ones that are equal in size. Sauté them, quartered lengthwise or sliced, with garlic in olive oil or broth until tender-crisp.

CABBAGE

Green cabbage gives you lots of folate, fiber, beta-carotene, and vitamin C, while red cabbage provides twice as much vitamin C. Its red color comes from antioxidants that protect against disease-causing free radicals. When cut, cabbage quickly loses nutrients. Cooking it al dente keeps its sweet taste.

NAPA CABBAGE

Napa cabbage, with its light green crinkly leaves, is an excellent source of folate and has nutrients strongly linked to cancer prevention. It is more flexible and less dense than regular green cabbage, so it can be used as a wrapper as you might a tortilla, and is especially good for Asian-style fillings.

CAULIFLOWER

White, green, and purple cauliflower all give you vitamins B5, B6, C, and folate, along with manganese essential for peak brain function and proper sugar metabolism. Serve this versatile crucifer in soups and stews; mashed, puréed, roasted, or steamed; or raw in crudités and salads. Heads should be firm, with no soft or brown spots on the curd.

dark greens

The strong flavor and deep color of these leafy greens means that they offer big health benefits. All are rich in carotenes and carotenoids. Cruciferous greens also contain important sulfur compounds.

MUSTARD GREENS
There are two types of mustard greens. The first has sharp-tasting, big, ruffled leaves, which are second only to collards in calcium content. These are best braised. The second kind, milder-tasting Asian varieties, have smaller leaves, rich in carotenes, that are tender enough to stir-fry.

BROCCOLI RABE
Use the leaves, florets, and all but the toughest part of this leafy green that is rich in beta-carotene. Boiling softens the bitter flavor of this crucifer as does the addition of a touch of lemon juice or vinegar in the dish.

SPINACH
A top source of heart-protective folate, carotenoids, iron, and bone-strengthening vitamin K, spinach is wildly versatile. Spinach can replace lettuce on a sandwich, or be mixed into meatloaf.

for more
on kale
see page 102

CHARD

Cook the shiny leaves and creamy, wide stems of Swiss chard separately to enjoy its earthy, tender, carotene-rich leaves plus mild-tasting fiber-rich crunch. The leaves cook like spinach, and the stems may be braised, or boiled and then sautéed. Ruby and rainbow chard stems may be too tough to eat.

KALE

Among crucifers, kale beats broccoli in beta-carotene and carotenoid content as well as in vitamin A and calcium. There are many types of kale. More tender types can be used for salads and all can be quickly and lightly braised in broth or wine for an easy and healthful side dish.

COLLARD GREENS

This soul food contains as much calcium in a serving as a glass of milk. It is also a powerhouse combination of sulfur compounds. For the sweetest flavor, steam or blanch the shredded leaves, then sauté or braise them with garlic or bacon.

salad greens

The most appealing salads include an assortment of greens. Using a variety makes salads healthier, too. Eating two cups of salad a day is a sure way to get good amounts of folate, vitamins A, C, and K, carotenes, minerals, and an array of the phytonutrients we need to stay healthy.

ROMAINE

Make romaine the heart of a salad—the folate in it will do your heart good. Chromium in its leaves helps to maintain healthy blood sugar levels. Cutting a head of romaine into long wedges and searing them on the grill creates a crisp center and smoky flavor that is wonderful served with a sprinkling of Parmesan shards.

RADICCHIO

The wine-red color and bitter flavor in this leafy chicory come from some of the same antioxidants found in eggplant and red berries. For a classic tri-color salad, combine radicchio with endive and watercress. Pan-Grilled Radicchio with Salsa Verde (page 135) shows how heat softens the bitterness and turns the radicchio leaves a warm brown color.

WATERCRESS

Adding peppery watercress to salads sharpens their flavor. Its zing comes from the same sulfur compounds found in broccoli and other crucifers. In addition, watercress contains calcium, vitamins A and K, and carotenoids. This surprisingly versatile green is also delicious stir-fried with garlic and ginger as a side dish.

ARUGULA

With just five calories in a cup, this zesty green rich in calcium and vitamin C is a smart choice. Arugula's bite tells you that it contains important sulfur-based anticancer phyto-chemicals—even more so in extra-sharp wild arugula. Arrange sliced tomatoes and mozzarella cheese on a bed of feathery arugula for a light meal.

onions & cousins

Eating alliums abundantly—from pungent garlic and onions to milder leeks and green onions—is a prescription for optimum health. The compounds that make their flavors indispensable in cooking also combat heart disease and high blood pressure and help improve blood cholesterol levels.

LEEKS

Leeks contain the same sulfides as other alliums that protect against cancer and thin the blood to help reduce the risk of strokes. They also contain carotenoids and vitamin A good for eye health. Sauté a chopped leek together with onions to give vegetable and bean soups more flavor.

GARLIC

Using garlic raw provides the most nutritional benefits, including anti-inflammatory, antibacterial, and antimicrobial powers. Let chopped garlic stand for 10 minutes to increase its powers and offset the heat of cooking, which diminishes them. Adding garlic later in cooking also helps retain its nutritional benefits.

GREEN ONIONS

Mild in flavor, these immature onions contain a small amount of the sulfur compounds founds in other alliums but they contain useful amounts of vitamin C and folate. These are the easiest kind of onion to eat raw, so add chopped green onions to salads and salsas or sauté them with spinach.

RED ONIONS

Studies have shown that red onions have a higher concentration of health-promoting substances in their outer layers than other types of onions and they are linked to a lower cancer risk. Cutting all onions 5–10 minutes before using releases more of their health-promoting compounds.

YELLOW ONIONS

Antioxidant compounds give onions their color. Onions are also rich in probiotics that nurture the good bacteria in your gut. An easy way to eat more onions is to sear thick slices in a dry heavy skillet or on the grill to serve as a side dish.

SHALLOTS

Blending the flavors of garlic and onion, shallots contain lesser amounts of the beneficial compounds found in both. Use them to add flavor to sauces, soups, stews, and vinaigrettes. Wrap whole shallots in foil and roast at 400°F (200°C) until soft. Serve with fish or veggie burgers, or mixed into egg salad.

roots, tubers & stalks

These roots and tubers, plus asparagus, an above-ground stalk, offer pleasingly assertive or sweet flavors. Most are good both cooked and served raw. Some contain enough sugar to satisfy your sweet tooth naturally. They all contain a useful amount of fiber.

SWEET POTATOES

The amount of vitamins A, C, B6, manganese, potassium, and beta-carotene in sweet potatoes varies, depending on whether their flesh is cream-color, yellow, or deep red-orange—the darker the flesh, the richer they are in phytonutrients. Bake sweet potatoes, then stir their soft flesh with a fork to enjoy the healthiest mashed potatoes.

RADISHES

Actually part of the brassica family, these roots contain known cancer-fighting substances. They are also rich in vitamin C, folic acid, and a host of minerals. Radishes' peppery bite is best preserved by eating them raw, and they can be added to salads or sandwiches or eaten on their own with a sprinkle of sea salt. To tame their taste, steam or sauté sliced radishes.

ASPARAGUS

Whether you prefer fat spears or slim, one cup of asparagus provides as much fiber as a slice of multigrain bread. This fiber includes a particular kind that supports good bacteria in your gut. Asparagus is also an excellent source of vitamins A and K and is rich in anti-inflammatory cancer-fighting compounds.

BEETS

The pigment that colors beets helps detoxify your body. To avoid staining your fingers, insert your hands into plastic sandwich bags while handling beets. The French serve shredded raw beets as a salad. Also try beet tops, which taste like Swiss chard. Steam them and serve drizzled with olive oil and lemon juice.

CARROTS

Cancer-preventive carotenoids and cholesterol-lowering fiber make carrots good for more than just your eyes. They are second only to beets in sugar content. Their fiber helps your body absorb this sweetness gradually. Serve raw, stir-fried, sautéed or roasted.

TOMATO

Tomatoes are rich in vitamins A and C, carotenes, and carotenoids, especially lycopene, a carotenoid believed to protect against heart disease and some types of cancer. As they redden, their carotenoid content increases. Refrigerating retards this, destroys flavor, and turns them mushy, so keep tomatoes on a shady counter. To avoid genetically engineered, ethylene-gassed tomatoes, buying organic is recommended.

SUMMER SQUASH

In summer, watch for crook-neck yellow squash, scallop-edged pattypan, thin-skinned lita, and round avocado and eight-ball squashes. Steaming them in water or broth preserves the modest amounts of vitamins A and C, along with beneficial minerals, in summer squashes.

ZUCCHINI

For the most nutrition, include the skin of zucchini when using it in recipes. And since you are eating the skin, it's always a good idea to choose organic. This summer squash is high in fiber, vitamins A and C, and potassium. Zucchini comes alive when you sauté it with garlic until it is just al dente, then shower on fresh basil.

vegetable fruits

We call all of these ingredients vegetables, but they contain the seeds of a plant, so botanically speaking they all are fruits. Perhaps that is why most of them combine nicely with fruit—try cucumber in mango salsa, green bell peppers and peaches in a green salad, and avocado accompanied by grapefruit sections.

for more
on tomatoes
see page
162

for info
on chiles
see page
72

AVOCADO

Creamy avocado is full of good-for-you fat
and a compound that reduces the risk of blood
clots. The buttery Hass variety—easily identified
by its pebbly skin— contains the highest amount
of these benefits. To enjoy avocado more
often, mash and spread it on toast when
making a sandwich and purée it into smoothies.

BELL PEPPER

Purple, red, orange, and yellow peppers
all are green ones allowed to ripen fully.
Besides sweetening their taste, ripening
also alters their nutrition—green
peppers that are high in vitamin C
become rich in vitamin A and
carotenoids as they turn bright colors.
For an antipasto, serve roasted peppers
drizzled with olive oil and lemon juice.

CUCUMBER

Cucumbers are nutritionally modest but filling. There are just
14 calories in a cup and their juiciness makes them help you feel
full. Select unwaxed cucumbers, preferably organic ones, so you
can enjoy them unpeeled. At the market, squeeze them to check
for freshness—cucumbers should be firm from end to end.

berries & grapes

Berries and grapes are so loaded with antioxidants that eating them daily is a smart practice. Include them in savory or sweet cooking in addition to eating them raw. For example, sauté pork medallions, deglaze the pan with red wine, add halved grapes, swirl in a pat of butter, and enjoy this rosy sauce with the pork.

GRAPES & RAISINS

Red and black grapes are the best choice—their skin contains the same health-supporting compounds found in red wine. Since both grapes and raisins are high in sugar, minimize snacking on them in favor of adding them to cereals, salads, and desserts. Bake focaccia topped with halved grapes and chopped fresh thyme or rosemary for a true Tuscan snack.

BLUEBERRIES

Bluberries are a powerful source of antioxidants that have been linked to improved memory. In addition, they are rich in flavonoids, which protect against cancer and contribute to heart health. Versatile, low in calories, and high in fiber, they are a must-have for a healthy lifestyle.

BLACKBERRIES

These plump berries are loaded with fiber—there is over seven grams in one cup. To use them regularly, top pancakes with blackberries simmered along with a little sugar, and include them with other berries when making a cobbler, crisp, or pie. Choose berries that are entirely black to ensure they are fully sweet—even a touch of purple makes them tart.

RASPBERRIES

Raspberries are amazingly rich in fiber: One cup contains nine grams, which is about one-third of a day's recommended fiber, together with an abundance of antioxidants. Fresh berries are delicate, and best served the day you buy them. If you must store them, spread them on a paper towel-lined baking sheet in one layer before refrigerating.

CRANBERRIES

Cranberries get their puckery taste from tannins, substances also found in red wine and tea. Their deep color tells you they contain other goodness, as well. To eat cranberries year-round while using less sugar, include dried cranberries in salads, trail mix, and alongside fresh or frozen ones in sauces, relish, or other dishes.

STRAWBERRIES

A strawberry's bright red color indicates an abundance of antioxidants helpful in protecting against cancer and giving support to short-term memory. Strawberries also contain lots of vitamin C and a good amount of fiber. Strawberries are often a big hit with kids, so keep them on hand for healthy snacking.

for more on
strawberries
see page 52

for more on
blueberries
see page 212

citrus

To perfume a room, simple peel any citrus fruit. The fragrant oils abundant in their skin also provide valuable health benefits. This makes including their juice or zest in recipes a good idea—using organic fruit, if possible. Nearly every kind of citrus contains compounds that are unique so eat a variety of them. Most fruits are at their peak from winter through spring.

CLEMENTINES

This orange-mandarin cross boasts health benefits similar to these fruits. Clementines are smaller than oranges and have deeper color. They are mostly seedless and easy to peel, making them popular with kids. A great snack, clementines are rich in vitamin C, calcium, and potassium.

LIMES

Limes, with similar health benefits to lemons, are an excellent source of vitamin C and a good source of folic acid, vitamin B6, potassium, and phytochemicals. Squeeze limes liberally into drinks and use to flavor and finish Asian and Latin American dishes whenever you can.

KUMQUATS

Kumquats are unique as the only citrus fruit you can eat whole, including the skin, which contains essential oils rich in antioxidants. Fresh kumquats provide high levels of flavonoid compounds, plus vitamins A and C and fiber. Slice them thinly and add them to salads and desserts.

TANGERINES

Tangerines, including petite mandarins, peel so easily that they are called "zipper fruits." Along with other antioxidants, they contain tangeretin, an anti-inflammatory phytochemical that helps thin the blood and protect against cancer. Whole mandarins, thinly sliced, are delicious baked on top of chicken breast or turkey cutlets.

LEMONS

A touch of their juice or zest gives nearly any dish a flavor boost along with cancer protection. Meyer lemons, a cross of lemon and mandarin, are so naturally sweet that you can use them to make unsweetened lemonade.

GRAPEFRUITS

White grapefruits, mainly from Florida, have the sweetest taste and plenty of good nutrition. Pink and red varieties add the benefits of colorful antioxidants. The best-tasting varieties are Star Ruby and Flame or Rio Red.

ORANGES

Along with an abundance of vitamin C and potassium, oranges are particularly rich in flavonoids, active compounds found mostly in citrus fruits. In all, their nutritional riches give oranges too many health benefits to list.

stone fruits

So-called because they contain a large pit, or "stone," in the center, stone fruits come to market in the late spring and summer. The more vibrantly colored they are, the more beneficial substances stone fruits contain—and in higher amounts. So favor golden peaches and nectarines over white, and choose oxheart cherries and the most intensely colored plums when you can.

PLUMS

From yellow and red to blue and green, plums offer a rainbow of colors, each rich in slightly different antioxidants. Sugar-loaded low-acid varieties lack the tart tang of older plum varieties. Roasting is a great way to cook this summer fruit.

PLUOTS

Aprium, plumcots, and pluots—all are slightly different versions of plum-apricot crosses and all boast similar health benefits of the original fruits. Pluots are perhaps the most popular and easy to find, and are good sources of vitamin A, vitamin C, potassium, and fiber. Their sweet-tart flavor is a unique treat, and worth seeking out.

NECTARINES

Nectarines and peaches are so botanically close that nectarines sometimes appear on a peach tree. Provided they show no green tinge, nectarines continue to ripen sitting on the kitchen counter. They are ready when they yield to pressure along the rim that circles them.

CHERRIES

The darker sweet cherries are, the richer they are in antioxidants. Sour cherries, sometimes called pie cherries, contain substances helpful for people with joint inflammation. Fresh, frozen, dried, or as juice, cherries can be used in both sweet and savory dishes alike.

PEACHES

The best peaches are local, tree-ripened, and eaten out of hand. They're good sources of vitamins A and C and contain valuable antioxidants, to ward off cancer; fiber, to protect the digestive system; and potassium, to help regulate blood pressure. Keep peaches at room temperature until they ripen and them eat them promptly; like tomatoes, peaches turn mushy when refrigerated.

APRICOTS

Eating fresh apricots raw is nutritionally best because when they are cooked or dried a valuable substance in them disappears. Under-ripe fruit gets softer and sweeter when kept at room temperature and its carotenoid content increases. The best tasting dried apricots are Blenheims from California.

tropical fruits

A seductive way to add fiber to your day, eating tropical fruits also provides unique health benefits, including some from enzymes that have important anti-inflammatory activity in your body. To best enjoy the aromatic qualities of tropical fruits, keep them on the counter unless they are already cut.

BANANAS

Bananas are so rich in potassium that eating just one benefits your blood pressure. They contain a probiotic compound that nurtures bacteria necessary for good gut health. Layer sliced banana on a peanut butter sandwich, dip it into melted dark chocolate, and slice and serve over hot breakfast cereal. For creamy and thick dairy-free smoothies, whirl in a banana.

MANGOES

Mangoes are a good source of carotenoids and fiber. A fully ripe one should bathe you in aroma and juice. When shopping for the fruit, go by feel—not color—since some varieties stay green when ripe. Use ripe mango in savory dishes. An unripe one makes good chutney. Use fresh or frozen mango in breakfast smoothies.

COCONUTS

Coconuts and their milk are high in saturated fats, but some experts support them as healthy because they help our immune system to defend against viruses and bacteria. Coconut is a good source of fiber and potassium so use dried coconut in granola and in baking, and sprinkle it on cereal. Use coconut milk in Asian-style dishes.

KIWI

A serving of kiwi contains more vitamin C than an orange, more potassium than a banana, and as much fiber as a bowl of oatmeal. Rock-hard kiwi are unripe and sharply sour. Held at room temperature until they soften slightly, they will taste mildly like wintergreen. Pureed kiwi makes a tangy sauce to serve with grilled halibut or salmon.

PAPAYAS

Squeezing lime juice on a wedge of ripe papaya heightens its tropical flavor. An enzyme in papayas is believed to reduce the risk of rheumatoid arthritis, and lung and color cancer. Papaya seeds look like little black pearls. Sprinkled on a salad they add a peppery flavor.

PINEAPPLES

Pineapples contain an enzyme that is anti-inflammatory and also helps digestion. Pineapples don't get sweeter after picking so look for a ripe one—it will feel heavy and be fragrant. (Forget about pulling a leaf out of the top; it's incorrect.) Use the versatile fruit in salsa for Latin-style fish dishes or whirled into smoothies.

PINTO BEANS

The speckled pattern on the skin of these beige beans disappears during cooking as pinto beans turn an even, rosy pink. The ideal choice when making refried beans or stuffing a burrito, velvety pinto beans are also good puréed, seasoned with cumin, oregano, and roasted garlic, and served as a fiber-rich dip.

LENTILS

Without soaking, protein-rich lentils cook in 20 to 40 minutes. Use flat, green lentils in soups or salads. Red and yellow split lentils are ideal for soups and Indian dal. Black belugas and green Le Puy lentils hold their shape, so think of them for salads.

fresh & dried legumes

In a plant-based diet, dried beans, lentils, and fresh or frozen peas are important protein sources. They are rich in fiber, too. With canned beans, watch their sodium content. Rinsing removes much of the salt, but adding it yourself to bean dishes made using dried beans is better than being stuck with what's in the can.

KIDNEY BEANS

Whether kidney beans are dark red or soft pink, the unique contrast between their firm skin and creamy inside makes them excellent in salads and soups. White kidney or cannellini beans, mashed with herbs and olive oil, make a delicious topping for crostini. The beans are a good source of molybdenum, a mineral that activates enzymes in the body.

ENGLISH PEAS

Fresh English peas, also called garden or green peas, are sugar-sweet when picked. They quickly turn starchy, so unless you can rush them from garden to pot like fresh corn, using frozen peas, always processed at their peak, makes sense. Peas are rich in calcium and a carotenoid that is particularly good for your eyes.

BLACK BEANS

Black beans are exceptionally versatile. Excellent in meatless chili, their firm yet creamy texture is ideal in salads and salsas. The intense, dark color of black beans, also called turtle beans, means they are loaded with important antioxidant phytochemicals.

SNOW PEAS

Besides color and crunch, snow peas add useful protein to a meatless stir-fry. Select pods with fresh-looking leaflets near their stem. They also should snap crisply when broken in half. To avoid overcooking, add snow peas to the pan later. When blanching, give them just a fast plunge in and out of the boiling water.

CHICKPEAS

Also called garbanzo beans, chickpeas are a multi-ethnic bean, delicious in Middle Eastern grain salads and hummus, Italian soups, and Spanish stews. Chickpeas are a good source of calcium, magnesium, potassium, and hard-to-find selenium.

SUGAR SNAP PEAS

A relative newcomer, sugar snap peas were introduced in 1976. Fresh sugar snaps look glossy and make a popping sound when opened. One cup contains 5 grams of fiber, more than a bowl of oatmeal.

whole grains

Studies show that few Americans eat enough fiber. Serving whole grains every day is an important—and delicious—way to change this. Their protein and the full feeling you get from eating them make whole grains fundamental to a plant-based diet. Choosing organically grown grains assures that they are not genetically engineered.

QUINOA

Light-textured and mildly earthy tasting, quinoa cooks in just 20 minutes. Particularly high in protein, this South American grain makes a good hot breakfast cereal, savory pilafs, and satisfying salads. Red quinoa used in place of bulgur makes great gluten-free tabbouleh.

BARLEY

Barley is frequently polished to remove most of the bran. Called pearl barley, it is healthfully high in cholesterol-lowering soluble fiber. Cook barley like oatmeal for breakfast, or make it into risotto for a healthy supper.

FARRO

Nutty, almost sweet tasting farro is an ancient, unhybridized form of wheat. Italians cook it whole—like rice and barley—or use ground farro to make excellent whole-wheat pasta. Eating farro in a salad is a nice introduction to this pleasant grain.

BULGUR

Middle Eastern cooks use bulgur—whole wheat that has been steamed, dried, and cracked—to make tabbouleh. Its pronounced flavor is also good in pilafs served alongside a main course. Bulgur is particularly high in fiber, with over 8 grams in a half-cup serving.

WHOLE-WHEAT FLOUR

Milled including the germ and bran, whole-wheat flour tastes more assertive than white and it can make baked goods weightier. Combining whole-wheat and white flour gives lighter results in baked goods and softens its taste. For dessert baking, try using whole-wheat pastry flour. For pasta, look for whole-wheat semolina.

POLENTA

To be whole-grain, cornmeal and polenta must be stone-ground. Only the ones made from yellow corn include the golden carotenoids that protect your eyes and heart. Made using milk, polenta makes a delicious morning porridge.

BROWN RICE

Brown whole-grain rice is a gluten-free staple in healthy eating. Fluffy brown jasmine and basmati have the same aromatic flavor as white. Nutty-tasting long-grain brown rice has more body. Medium-grain brown rice has a pleasing chewy texture.

OATS

In the morning, serve rolled oats, thick-cut old-fashioned oats, or nubbly steel-cut oats. Use regular or quick-cooking oatmeal—both provide the same amounts of healthful soluble and insoluble fiber. Avoid instant oatmeal, which has minimal fiber or flavor.

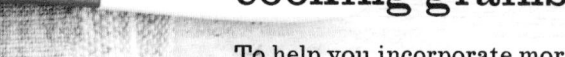

cooking grains

To help you incorporate more whole grains into your diet, here are six techniques for cooking versatile grains to use in any meal.

BASIC COOKED QUINOA

Rinse 1 part quinoa with cold water and drain through a fine-mesh sieve. Repeat 3 times, then place in a saucepan. Add 2 parts water and a pinch of salt and bring to a boil. Cover and simmer until the water is absorbed, about 15 minutes. Turn off the heat and let stand at least 5 minutes before using.

BASIC COOKED BARLEY

In a saucepan, bring 4 parts water to a boil. Add 1 part pearl barley and a pinch of salt and simmer until the grains are tender, about 45 minutes. Drain before using.

BASIC COOKED FARRO

In a saucepan, combine 1 part rinsed semi-pearled farro with 2 parts water and a pinch of salt. Bring to a boil, then cover and simmer until the grains are tender and the water is absorbed, about 25 minutes.

BASIC COOKED BULGUR

In a saucepan, combine 1 part medium-grain bulgur and 2 parts water. Bring to a boil, then cover and simmer until the grains are tender, 10–12 minutes.

BASIC SOFT POLENTA

In a saucepan, bring 5 parts broth or water to a boil along with a large pinch of salt. Slowly whisk in 1 part coarse polenta. Simmer, stirring often, until the polenta pulls away from the sides of the pan, 20–45 minutes.

BASIC COOKED BROWN RICE

In a saucepan, combine 1 part rice, 2 parts water, and a pinch of salt. Bring to a boil, then cover and simmer until the rice is tender and the water is absorbed, 45–60 minutes.

lean protein

Protein is essential for maintaining muscle and repairing damaged DNA in your body. So besides eating lean cuts of poultry, beef, or pork, have fish or seafood at least twice a week, particularly ones that contain omega-3s. When grilling any type of protein, marinate it first. This helps to prevent the formation of toxic substances in addition to adding flavor and moisture.

POULTRY

Chicken's white meat is more versatile, but turkey breast has more flavor. Turkey is also slightly leaner and it has less saturated fat than chicken. A sturdier bird, turkey is raised without hormones and using fewer antibiotics, as well. Both chicken and turkey are good sources of tryptophan, the mood-boosting amino acid that also helps sleep.

PORK

Only turkey breast is leaner than pork tenderloin. To help keep this tender cut moist, roast it whole or sauté it in medallions and serve it with a quick pan sauce. In commercially raised pork, antibiotics, stressful living conditions, and the environmental pollution created are concerns. Buying organic or local and humanely raised pork can avoid this.

BEEF

Eating lean beef in moderation provides needed vitamin B-12, zinc, and iron. When it is grass-fed, beef also contains omega-3s and it is leaner than corn-fed, conventionally raised beef. Plus, grass-fed cattle are antibiotic-free and humanely treated. Combine beef with lots of vegetables for a healthy dish.

SALMON

Wild salmon is the food richest in omega-3 fat. Fresh wild salmon is sustainable but it can be costly, so consider canned—most of it is wild Alaska salmon. Try using a can of skinless, boneless salmon to replace the bulgur in tabbouleh, for example. The health benefits from salmon are so important that experts agree that eating farmed is worthwhile if that fits your budget.

SHRIMP

Eating shrimp is another way to get important omega-3s. Although it appears to be fresh, most shrimp is previously frozen and treated with sulfites. To avoid this preservative, ask your fishmonger or read the packaging. Look for shrimp caught wild or farmed in the U.S. Watch, too, for small, sweet, cold-water shrimp from Maine, Canada, or the northern Pacific.

WHITE FISH

Cod, halibut, and black cod—actually sablefish—have at least some omega-3 fat and are rated as Best Choices for sustainability by the Monterey Bay Aquarium's Seafood Watch. Their mild flavor and adaptability in cooking help to make eating fish a couple of times a week appealing. Tiny anchovies are also considered sustainable and boast omega-3 fatty acids and some calcium.

dairy

Eggs, milk, yogurt, and cheese are well-priced sources of complete protein, but choosing dairy products with low amounts of saturated fat is best. Eating dairy foods is also the easiest way to get the calcium you need. Including a small amount of strongly flavored cheese in grain and bean dishes complements their protein and gives a flavor boost.

EGGS

A whole egg provides 6 grams of top-quality protein. The white contains half an egg's protein, while the rest is in the yolk, along with brain-protecting choline. The yolk's color comes from carotenoids, which are important for eye health. Organic eggs are an antibiotic- and hormone-free food. Using eggs laid by pastured hens supports humane treatment.

MILK

A cup of milk delivers nearly one-third of the calcium an adult needs daily for healthy bones, plus vitamins D and K and magnesium that help your body use it. Using reduced-fat (2 percent) and low-fat (1 percent) milk saves calories and significantly reduces saturated fat.

YOGURT

To keep your gut happy and healthy, yogurt must deliver cultures that are both live and active. Always check the label for this. Drink yogurt in a smoothie, combine it with cucumber and mint for a refreshing sauce, or add a dollop of higher-protein, thick Greek-style yogurt to soups and fruit-based desserts.

BUTTERMILK

Buttermilk is made by culturing low fat or skim milk with friendly bacteria. The enzymes these bacteria produce have a tenderizing effect in marinades. Buttermilk lightens pancakes, waffles, and dessert batters and adds a pleasant tang. Use it to make lean, fluffy mashed potatoes and smart, creamy salad dressings.

PARMESAN

Cheesemongers consider authentic Italian Parmigiano-Reggiano the queen of cheeses. Made using partially skimmed milk from grass-fed cows, it is particularly digestible compared to other cheeses. Parmesan from Argentina is a well-priced alternative. Edible Parmigiano rind simmered in a pot of minestrone adds savory umami flavor.

PECORINO

An Italian sheep's milk cheese, the best pecorino comes from near Rome or Sardinia. Its sharp, salty flavor is good with pasta and in lasagna. Mix grated pecorino into meatloaf or chip off chunks and nibble them with a ripe pear. For the most flavor, buy a hunk of pecorino to use as needed.

FETA

Feta is usually sheep's milk cheese pickled in brine, although there are goat and cow's milk versions, too. Feta in chunks should be sold and stored bathed in brine. Crumbled feta may be sold dry. Look for reduced-fat feta in supermarkets. A little crumbled over a salad or blended into turkey burgers adds tangy flavor.

PISTACHIOS

Pistachios get their green color from chlorophyll, which may help to protect against certain cancers and to reduce inflammation. For snacking, a serving—1 ounce of shelled nuts—is a generous 49 pistachios. Look for shelled pistachios at natural food stores.

CASHEWS

Cashews are slightly lower in calories than other nuts. They do contain a fair amount of saturated fat, so serving them as a crunchy element in recipes may a better idea than overindulging by snacking on them. Raw cashews whirled with water, then strained, make a rich, dairy-free milk.

SESAME SEEDS

Rich in calcium, sesame seeds also contain a substance that lowers cholesterol in the liver as well as in the blood. To bring out their flavor, whirl sesame seeds in a dry, heavy skillet until fragrant. Asian toasted sesame oil adds deep, nutty flavor and extra nutrition to Asian-style dishes.

nuts & seeds

The monounsaturated fat in nuts and seeds makes them good for your heart and brain. Eating them also helps you feel satisfied. To keep calories under control, when snacking on nuts, measure out one serving before you start munching.

WALNUTS

Walnuts contain a good amount of omega-3s. Roasted walnut oil drizzled on steamed vegetables gives rich flavor and aroma while adding health benefits. Whirling walnuts in a food processor with walnut oil and a pinch of salt makes delicious nut butter.

PINE NUTS

This protein-rich, rice grain–shaped nut really comes from pine trees. Mediterranean pine nuts have a sweeter taste and softer texture than pine nuts from China. Besides pesto, use pine nuts in green or grain salads to add extra fiber and healthy unsaturated fats.

PUMPKIN SEEDS

Slightly bitter pumpkin seeds blend nicely with other nuts in granola and trail mix. Also use them on top of muffins and tea cakes. A 1-ounce serving, about ¼ cup, contains 8 grams of protein. Pumpkin seeds contain a substance that helps prevent and control an enlarged prostate.

ALMONDS

Compared to other nuts, almonds contain the highest amount of monounsaturated fat and the most fiber. A quarter-cup of almonds contains more protein than an egg. The nutrition in the skin of whole almonds makes them the best choice when you can use them. Almond milk is an excellent choice for dairy-free cooking.

good fats & sweeteners

Yes, fats are high in calories. But some contain anti-inflammatory fatty acids that our body cannot produce and that are essential to our well-being. Using fats in moderation is smart. Sweeteners are a luxury we all deserve on occasion. Used judiciously, these less refined ones include some nutritional goodness or are gentler on blood sugar levels than refined sugar.

GRAPESEED OIL

High in an essential fatty acid the body cannot make, grapeseed oil has a high smoke point, which makes it good for stir-frying, sautéing, and baking. Chefs use this neutral-tasting oil for salad dressings as well as in cooking.

OLIVE OIL

Antioxidants in extra-virgin olive oil help raise good cholesterol and lower bad cholesterol in your blood. The more peppery it tastes, the more of these polyphenols the oil contains. Extra-virgin olive oil is best used in dressings and for drizzling. Heat destroys its antioxidants, so limit its cooking use to quick sautés. Regular olive oil and light olive oil have a high smoke point best for sautéing.

CANOLA OIL

Its neutral taste and favorable omega-3 to omega-6 ratio make canola oil good for salad dressings, sautéing and baking. Using cold-pressed or expeller-pressed canola oil is preferable. Spectrum Naturals High Heat Canola is particularly well suited for cooking.

HONEY

Honey is thirty-five percent sweeter than sugar, so adjust accordingly when using it in baking and cooking. The darker the honey, the stronger it tastes. Wildflower honey's neutral taste is ideal for many dishes. Raw honey is recommended because it contains enzymes and phytonutrients destroyed by pasteurization and filtering.

AGAVE

This liquid sweetener made from a plant related to aloe has a low glycemic index and is twenty-five times sweeter than sugar, so a little goes a long way in recipes. Golden light agave tastes neutrally sweet. Caramel-colored dark agave tastes warm and mellow. Both are good in desserts, drinks, and sauces.

MAPLE SYRUP

Maple syrup contains calcium, potassium, zinc and other minerals. The mild taste of Grade A Fancy syrup goes well with apples, strawberries, and other fruit. Grade B Dark maple syrup has an almost smoky, intense flavor. Use this less expensive grade for hot cereals, in baking, and for glazing sweet potatoes. Dark fudge sauce made with maple syrup is a special treat.

working with herbs

In general, only the leaves from fresh herbs are used in cooking. Following is a primer on how to prep them for recipes.

LARGE-LEAFED HERBS

Fresh herbs that boast large or broad leaves, such as basil, sage, and mint, can be either slivered or chopped for recipes. Use your fingers to pull off the leaves one at a time. Stack 5 or 6 leaves on top of one another, then roll the stack lengthwise into a tight cylinder. Using a chef's knife, cut the leaves crosswise into narrow slivers. To chop the herbs, gather the slivers into a pile and rock the blade over them to cut into small pieces.

SMALL-LEAFED HERBS

For herbs such as cilantro, parsley, and tarragon, pull the leaves from the stems one at a time. Heap the leaves together on a cutting board. Rock the blade of a chef's knife back and forth briefly over the leaves to chop coarsely. For finely chopped, continue to re-gather the leaves and rock the knife over them making small, even pieces. For minced, keep chopping until the pieces are as fine as possible.

BRANCHED OR WOODY HERBS

Remove the petal-like leaves from thyme or oregano by gently pulling your thumb and index finger together down the stems. Gather the leaves on a cutting board and follow the instructions for Small-Leafed Herbs (above) to chop or mince.

GENERAL TIPS

- Choose bunches with bright green, fragrant leaves

- Avoid bunches with wilted or discolored leaves, or pluck these from your garden plot

- Rinse herbs just before using and pat dry gently with paper towels

BASIL

Sweet, spicy Genovese basil and pungent Thai basil with its complex citrus, anise, and mint notes are both rich in antimicrobial and anti-inflammatory benefits. Because the aromatic compounds providing these benefits are volatile, add basil late in the cooking process to preserve them and get full flavor.

MINT

Sweet, mild spearmint is soothing, while bitter, sharp peppermint is stimulating. Both help to protect against the bacteria associated with ulcers.

CILANTRO

Widely used in Mexico, the Middle East, and South Asian cooking, cilantro is rich in antioxidants, plus antimicrobials that can protect against salmonella. Sprinkle cilantro on sliced oranges and on buttery carrots. Heat diminishes its flavor so add it later in chili and other cooked dishes.

fresh herbs

The same phytochemical compounds that give herbs their fragrance and flavor also give them proven health benefits. In cooking, use an array of herbs to get the full variety of their powers. Dried herbs quickly lose fragrance, flavor, and health powers, so from a nutritional standpoint, use fresh when possible.

PARSLEY

Flat-leaf or Italian parsley tastes better than curly and it contains more phytochemicals. A main ingredient in tabbouleh and Italian salsa verde, you can also use parsley to make gremolata by combining it with garlic, citrus zest, and capers to serve sprinkled on baked fish or lamb shanks.

OREGANO

This Mediterranean staple, which gives familiar flavor to Italian red sauce and Greek salad, has the highest antioxidant level of all herbs. When fresh oregano leaves are tough, use dried instead. Keep both pungent Greek oregano and faintly minty Mexican oregano on hand.

spices

Fragrant and vibrantly colored, spices have potent health benefits. To maximize their benefits, whenever possible, purchase spices whole and then grind them just before use. Buy spices in the smallest amounts you can, as they lose flavor, fragrance, and nutrients over time.

MUSTARD SEEDS

A brassica related to cabbage and broccoli, mustard seeds contain the same cancer-preventive substances the full-grown plants contain. Their mild heat and nutty flavor enhance vegetable dishes. Brown or black mustard seeds are best in cooking; yellow ones are great for pickling.

CAYENNE

Most cayenne pepper registers 35,000–50,000 on the Scoville (or heat) scale—hot, but not incendiary. If you don't like a lot of heat, you'll still see how a tiny pinch of cayenne pepper simply brightens the flavor in many types of dishes.

CHILE FLAKES

This fiery spice is the seeds and flakes of small dried red chiles. Like fresh chiles, they contain capsaicin, which stimulates endorphins and is beneficial to metabolism. Just a small amount adds bright heat to dishes.

TURMERIC

Golden turmeric contains one of nature's most potent anti-inflammatories. Since it has an unfamiliar, bitter taste, many cooks blend it with other spices or use curry powder containing turmeric. Add a pinch of turmeric to tomato sauce or a pot of lentils, and sprinkle it on cooked carrots.

GINGER

This warming spice has so many health benefits that Indians call it the universal remedy. Asian cooks favor using fresh ginger. Grating it on a rasp helps it blend into dishes nicely. North African and Middle Eastern recipes usually call for dried.

CUMIN

The seed of a member of the parsley family, cumin has a sharp, musky flavor and is used liberally in Indian, North African, and Latin cooking. Studies have shown that cumin may boost immune health and enhance digestion and it is a rich source of iron.

CINNAMON

Most cinnamon today is actually cassia, the bark from a tree growing in Vietnam and China, rather than true cinnamon from Ceylon. Cinnamon's distinctive flavor and fragrance works well in both sweet and savory dishes. Cinnamon helps to control blood sugar levels, so use both kinds liberally.

PAPRIKA

Spanish paprika, called pimentón, is darker and tastes more pungent than the Hungarian kind. Both come in sweet and hot varieties but pimentón has a smoked taste that is great with vegetables.

spice basics

Spices are easy to work with, but require a little care to retain maximum flavor and aroma. To ensure freshness and optimium nutrition, get them from a quality source that has a high turnover.

TOASTING SPICES

To intensify their flavor, put whole spices (such as mustard seeds, cumin seeds, and broken cinnamon sticks) in a dry frying pan over medium heat. Stir constantly until the spices are fragrant and a shade or two darker, 30 seconds to 1 minute. Pour the spices onto a plate to stop the cooking and let cool for about 10 minutes before grinding.

GRINDING SPICES

For grinding small quantities of spices, use a mortar and pestle. For larger amounts, use a small electric coffee grinder reserved only for grinding spices. Grind only the amount you need for a recipe.

COOKING WITH SPICES

Many recipes call for heating ground spices in a small amount of oil prior to incorporating them into a recipe to bring out their flavor. Called "blooming," this also helps spices to blend more readily with other ingredients.

STORING SPICES

Keep spices in tightly closed containers in a cool, dark place that is ideally not beside the stove. If you buy spices in bulk, purchase glass spice jars for storing. Whole spices will last for about 1 year. Ground spices keep for about 6 months.

fruit & vegetable elixirs

Drinking fresh juice helps boost overall heath and well-being, offering vitamins, minerals, and phytochemicals that are easy for the body to absorb. Using a juice extractor or high-speed blender makes raw fruits and vegetables easier to digest. In addition, drinking raw fruit and vegetable juices can help keep you hydrated, providing an energy boost throughout the day. Try these ten favorite combinations, or customize your own.

Pomegranate-Blueberry

Powerful antioxidant tonic that may help reduce cancer risk.

1 cup (6 oz/185 g) pomegranate seeds

2 cups (8 oz/250 g) blueberries

Agave nectar (optional)

In a juice extractor, juice the pomegranate seeds and blueberries. Taste the juice for sweetness and add a little agave if needed.

Makes about 1 cup (8 fl oz/250 ml)

Tomato, Celery, Cucumber & Carrot

Reduces cancer risk and boosts your complexion.

10 tomatoes

2 celery ribs

2 Persian cucumbers

2 carrots

Juice of 1 lemon

Core and quarter the tomatoes. Dice the celery and cucumbers. Chop the carrots. Put the tomatoes, celery, cucumbers, carrots, and lemon juice in a high-speed blender and process until smooth.

Makes about 4 cups (32 fl oz/1 l)

Orange, Celery & Carrot

Reduces cholesterol and helps prevent cancer.

4 navel oranges

4 celery ribs

8 carrots

Peel and quarter the oranges. In a juice extractor, juice the oranges followed by the celery ribs and carrots.

Makes about $2\frac{1}{4}$ cups (18 fl oz/560 ml)

Pear, Apple & Greens

Builds bones and strengthens the immune system.

1 pear

1 apple

4 oz (125 g) rainbow chard

2 oz (60 g) fresh spinach

$\frac{1}{2}$ cup ($\frac{3}{4}$ oz/20 g) chopped flat-leaf parsley

Halve and core the pear and the apple, and chop into chunks. Separate the stems and large veins from the chard leaves and coarsely chop. Put the pear, apple, chard leaves and stems, spinach, and parsley in a high-speed blender and process until smooth. Dilute with water, if desired.

Makes about 4 cups (32 fl oz/1 l)

Beet-Orange

Detoxifies and supports your immune system.

4 navel oranges
3 red beets

Peel and quarter the oranges. Scrub, trim, and quarter the beets. In a juice extractor, juice the oranges and beets.

Makes about 2$^1/_2$ cups (20 fl oz/625 ml)

Watermelon-Lime

Hydrates and infuses vitamins into your system.

1 seedless watermelon (about 2 lb/1 kg)
2 limes
2 teaspoons honey

Peel and chop the watermelon into small chunks. Peel, quarter, and seed the limes. Put the watermelon chunks, lime quarters, and honey in a blender and process until smooth. Dilute with water, if desired.

Makes about 4 cups (32 fl oz/1 l)

Honeydew-Kiwi

Boosts the immune system and helps balance electrolytes.

$^1/_2$ honeydew melon
4 kiwis
1 lime
$^1/_2$ tablespoon agave nectar, plus more if needed

Peel and seed the melon and cut it into chunks. Peel and quarter the kiwis. Peel, quarter, and seed the lime.

Put the melon, kiwis, lime, and agave in a high-speed blender and process until smooth. Dilute with water, if desired. Taste for sweetness and add a little more agave if needed.

Makes 5$^1/_2$ cups (44 fl oz/1.35)

Mango-Lime

Provides beneficial enzymes that have an anti-inflammatory effect.

3 mangoes
1 lime

Peel the mangoes, cut into large chunks, and discard the pits. Peel, quarter, and seed the lime.

Place the mangoes, lime quarters, and $^1/_2$ cup (4 fl oz/ 125 ml) water in a high-speed blender and process until smooth.

Makes 1$^1/_2$ cups (12 fl oz/375 ml)

Tomato-Pepper-Cucumber

Helps protect against heart disease and boost the immune system.

2 red bell peppers
1 tomato
1 Persian cucumber
$^1/_2$ jalapeño
Splash of balsamic vinegar

Halve the bell peppers, remove the seeds and ribs, and roughly chop. Quarter and core the tomato. Slice the cucumber. Mince the chile.

Put the peppers, tomato, cucumber, chile, vinegar, and $^1/_2$ cup (4 fl oz/125 ml) water in a high-speed blender and process until smooth.

Makes about 2 cups (16 fl oz/500 ml)

Wheatgrass-Carrot

Quickly delivers vitamins, minerals, and detoxifying substances.

1 container of wheatgrass
(about 1 cup/1 oz/30 g when trimmed)
4 carrots

Cut off the wheatgrass at the roots. In a juice extractor, juice the wheatgrass and carrots.

Makes about $^3/_4$ cup (6 fl oz/180 ml)

breakfast

This smoothie couldn't be simpler: just whirl together five superfoods in a blender with ice cubes and you have a balanced breakfast with loads of protein, fiber, and phytochemicals, and you'll have great energy and nutrition before you even leave for work.

Banana-Strawberry-Almond Smoothie

MAKES 2 SERVINGS

1 ripe banana

1 cup (4 oz/125 g) strawberries

1 cup (8 fl oz/250 ml) cranberry juice

1 cup (8 oz/250 g) nonfat plain yogurt

2 tablespoons whole natural almonds

$1/2$ cup (4 oz/125 g) ice cubes

Peel and slice the banana. Hull the strawberries and halve them lengthwise.

In a blender, combine the banana, strawberries, cranberry juice, yogurt, almonds, and ice cubes. Blend until frothy and thoroughly blended.

Divide between 2 tall glasses and serve right away.

Note: Turn to pages 48–49 for more smoothie ideas.

Fresh mango, cranberry juice, and creamy yogurt, blended together with ice cubes, make an unusual and refreshing breakfast drink. Mango is an excellent source of beta-carotene, and both mangoes and cranberries contain vitamin C.

Mango-Yogurt Smoothie

MAKES 2 SERVINGS

1 ripe mango

1 cup (8 fl oz/250 ml) sweetened
cranberry juice

1 cup (8 oz/250 g) nonfat
plain yogurt

$1/2$ cup (4 oz/125 g) ice cubes

To cut the mango, stand the fruit on one of its narrow sides, with the stem end facing you. Using a sharp knife, and positioning the blade about 1 inch (2.5 cm) from the stem, cut down the length of the fruit, just brushing the large, lengthwise pit. Repeat the cut on the other side of the pit. One at a time, holding each half cut side up, score the flesh in a grid pattern, forming 1/4-inch (6-mm) cubes and stopping just short of the skin. Push against the skin side to force the cubes outward, then cut across the base of the cubes to free them. Measure out 1 cup (6 oz/185 g) mango cubes; reserve the remainder for another use.

In a blender, combine the 1 cup mango cubes, cranberry juice, yogurt, and ice cubes. Blend until frothy and thoroughly blended.

Divide between 2 tall glasses and serve right away.

The beneficial bacteria in plain yogurt are thought to boost the immune system, increase the absorption of nutrients, and keep the intestinal tract healthy. To ensure optimum benefit, choose unsweetened yogurt that lists live and active cultures on the label.

Carrot-Pineapple Smoothie

MAKES 2 SERVINGS

2 cups (12 oz/375 g) frozen
pineapple chunks

$^1/_2$ cup (4 fl oz/125 ml) carrot juice

1 cup (8 oz/250 g) nonfat
plain yogurt

$^1/_2$ cup (4 oz/125 g) ice cubes

In a blender, combine the pineapple and carrot juice. Process until the mixture is smooth, 30–45 seconds. Add the yogurt and ice cubes and process until frothy and thoroughly blended, about 20 seconds longer.

Divide between 2 tall glasses and serve right away.

This crunchy, lightly sweetened nut-and-seed granola is easy to make and lower in fat and sugar than the typical cereal you see in stores. Serve it with yogurt and vitamin-packed blueberries for a great start to the day.

Homemade Granola with Blueberries & Yogurt

MAKES 6 SERVINGS

2 cups (6 oz/185 g) old-fashioned rolled oats

$1/2$ cup ($1^1/2$ oz/45 g) raw wheat germ

$1/4$ cup (1 oz/30 g) coarsely chopped walnuts

$1/4$ cup ($3/4$ oz/20 g) sesame seeds

$1/4$ cup (1 oz/30 g) shredded sweetened coconut

$1/4$ cup ($1^1/4$ oz/40 g) raw hulled pumpkin seeds

Pinch of salt

3 tablespoons honey

2 tablespoons grapeseed or canola oil

1 teaspoon ground cinnamon

2 cups (16 oz/500 g) nonfat plain Greek-style yogurt

2 cups (8 oz/250 g) blueberries

Preheat the oven to 400°F (200°C).

In a large bowl, combine the oats, wheat germ, walnuts, sesame seeds, coconut, pumpkin seeds, and salt and stir to mix. Spread the mixture in an even layer on a large rimmed baking sheet. Bake, stirring occasionally, until crisp and golden, about 15 minutes. Transfer to a large plate to cool. (The cooled granola will keep at room temperature in an airtight container for up to 1 week.)

In a small saucepan over low heat, combine the honey, oil, and cinnamon and cook, stirring, just until the mixture is warm and well blended, about 2 minutes. Add half of the honey mixture to the bowl with the granola and toss to combine and coat thoroughly. Add just enough of the remaining honey mixture so that the granola clumps slightly but is not soupy. Reserve any extra for another use.

Divide the yogurt among individual bowls. Top with the granola and blueberries and serve right away.

Strawberries Pack a Punch

Strawberries' bright red color indicates an abundance of antioxidants helpful in protecting against cancer and supporting short-term memory. They also contain lots of vitamin C and a good amount of fiber. Commercial producers of conventionally grown strawberries use toxic chemicals to protect this fragile fruit, so consider using organic, whether you're buying fresh or frozen berries.

Fresh strawberries taste best in early spring through summer, but frozen fruit captures their goodness at other times of the year. Stir a teaspoon of honey or sugar into a bowl of sliced fresh berries and watch them create their own syrup.

Four Ways to Use Fresh Strawberries

Honeyed Strawberries

In a small saucepan over low heat, warm ¼ cup (2 fl oz/60 ml) orange blossom or wildflower honey, stirring, until thinned but not hot, about 1 minute. Remove from the heat. Add 2 tablespoons fresh lemon juice and 1 cup (4 oz/125 g) hulled and sliced strawberries and stir until blended. Cover and let stand at room temperature until ready to serve. Serve with pancakes or waffles. Serves 4.

Strawberry Sauce

In a food processor, combine 2 cups hulled strawberries and 2–3 tablespoons honey (depending on the sweetness of the berries) and pulse just until the berries are puréed. Pour the purée through a fine-mesh sieve set over a bowl, pressing the purée through the sieve with a wooden spoon and leaving the seeds behind. Stir in 1–2 teaspoons fresh lemon juice to brighten the flavor. Cover and refrigerate for up to 5 days. Serve as a topping for hot breakfast cereal or desserts. Makes 2 cups (16 fl oz/500 ml).

Roasted Berries

In a wide, shallow baking dish, combine 2 cups (8 oz/250 g) hulled strawberries, ½ cup (2 oz/60 g) blueberries, ¼ cup maple syrup, and 1 tablespoon fresh orange juice and toss to coat. Spread the berries into an even layer. Roast the berries in a 450°F (230°C) oven until they just begin to soften, 5–7 minutes. Serve warm with crisp, whole-grain cookies or low-fat cake or over low-fat frozen yogurt. Makes about 2½ cups (20 fl oz/750 ml).

Dark Chocolate–Dipped Strawberries

Place 8 oz (250 g) chopped bittersweet chocolate in a heatproof bowl. Place over (not touching) barely simmering water in a saucepan and heat, stirring occasionally, until melted and smooth. Remove from the heat. One at a time, dip 12–16 strawberries about two-thirds of the way into the chocolate and then set on a sheet pan lined with waxed paper. Refrigerate until the chocolate is set, about 15 minutes or up to 2 hours. Makes 12–16 dipped strawberries.

Oatmeal is always a nutritious choice for the morning. Here it is topped with fresh raspberries in fragrant almond syrup for a new twist on an old favorite. Cooking the oats in nonfat milk, rather than water, produces a rich, creamy texture.

Old-Fashioned Oatmeal with Almond-Raspberry Compote

MAKES 4 SERVINGS

$1/2$ cup (4 oz/125 g) sugar

2 teaspoons fresh lemon juice

$1/4$ teaspoon pure almond extract

$1^1/2$ cups (6 oz/190 g) raspberries

4 cups (32 fl oz/1 l) nonfat milk

$1/4$ teaspoon sea salt

2 cups (6 oz/185 g) old-fashioned rolled oats

In a saucepan over low heat, combine the sugar and $1/2$ cup (4 fl oz/125 ml) water and cook, stirring, until the sugar dissolves. Remove from the heat and pour the sugar syrup into a heatproof bowl. Stir in the lemon juice and almond extract. Let the syrup cool to room temperature. Gently stir in the raspberries and set aside.

In a heavy saucepan over medium-high heat, stir together the milk and salt and bring to a boil. Slowly stir in the oats. Reduce the heat to medium and cook at a gentle boil, uncovered, stirring often, until the oatmeal is soft and the milk is absorbed, about 5 minutes. Adjust the heat as needed to keep the oatmeal boiling gently. Remove from the heat, cover, and let stand for 3 minutes.

Spoon the hot oatmeal into individual bowls and top each one with the raspberries, dividing them evenly. Serve right away.

In Italy, breakfast polenta, called "polentina," is a creamier, looser form of polenta than is served at other times of the day. Top the whole-grain cereal with sliced bananas and maple syrup for a novel alternative to traditional oatmeal.

Maple-Banana Breakfast Polenta

MAKES 4 SERVINGS

$1^2/_3$ cups (13 fl oz/410 ml) nonfat milk, or more as needed

$1^1/_2$ tablespoons sugar

Fine sea salt

$3/_4$ cup (5 oz/155 g) polenta

2 ripe bananas, peeled and sliced

$1/_2$ cup ($5^1/_2$ fl oz/170 ml) pure Grade B maple syrup, warmed

In a large, heavy saucepan over medium-high heat, combine $1^2/_3$ cups (13 fl oz/410 ml) water and the milk, sugar, and $1/_4$ teaspoon salt and bring to a boil. Reduce the heat to very low and, when the liquid is barely simmering, drizzle in the polenta in a slow, thin stream, whisking constantly in the same direction until all the grains have been absorbed and the mixture is smooth and free of lumps. Switch to a wooden spoon and stir thoroughly every 1–2 minutes until the polenta is loose and creamy, about 15 minutes. (For thicker polenta, cook for up to 30 minutes.) Add a little more water and/or milk if the polenta gets too stiff; this should be a very liquid mixture.

Ladle the polenta into individual bowls. Distribute the bananas over the top. Drizzle with the warm maple syrup and serve right away.

Cinnamon-flavored whole wheat batter produces waffles with a crunchy texture and a nutty taste. They're irresistible topped with vitamin-packed, honey-sweetened berries. Serve these for a weekend breakfast and your family will probably not guess that they're healthy.

Whole-Wheat Waffles with Honeyed Strawberries

MAKES 4 SERVINGS

1 cup (5 oz/155 g) whole-wheat flour

$1/2$ cup ($2^1/_2$ oz/75 g) unbleached all-purpose flour

2 tablespoons wheat bran

1 tablespoon baking powder

1 teaspoon ground cinnamon

$1/2$ teaspoon fine sea salt

$1^1/_2$ cups (12 fl oz/375 ml) nonfat milk

2 large eggs

2 tablespoons grapeseed or canola oil, plus more for brushing

2 tablespoons wildflower or orange blossom honey

Honeyed Strawberries (page 53)

In a large bowl, whisk together the flours, bran, baking powder, cinnamon, and salt. In a large glass measuring pitcher, whisk together the milk, eggs, and the 2 tablespoons oil until blended. Add the honey to the milk mixture and whisk until blended. Make a well in the center of the dry ingredients and add the milk mixture. Stir just until blended; do not overmix. The batter will be thick.

Preheat the oven to 200°F (95°C). Preheat a waffle iron for 5 minutes, then brush with oil. Ladle about $1/2$ cup (4 fl oz/125 ml) of the batter into the center of the waffle iron, and spread with a small spatula to fill all the holes. Close the waffle iron and cook until the steam stops escaping from the sides and the top opens easily, 4–5 minutes, or according to the manufacturer's directions.

Transfer the waffle to a warmed platter and keep warm in the oven. Repeat with the remaining batter. Serve the waffles with the honeyed strawberries.

Sweet potatoes are a great source of beta-carotene and are full of fiber. Here, they star along with walnuts in a modern take on traditional pancakes that are dense with nutrition and full of autumn flavors. If you like, serve with Sautéed Apples (page 61).

Sweet Potato Pancakes with Walnuts

MAKES 6 SERVINGS

2 sweet potatoes, scrubbed but not peeled

2 tablespoons unsalted butter

1 1/2 cups (12 fl oz/375 ml) nonfat milk

2 large eggs

2 tablespoons brown sugar

1 1/2 teaspoons pure vanilla extract

1 cup (5 oz/155 g) whole-wheat flour

1/2 cup (2 1/2 oz/75 g) unbleached all-purpose flour

1 tablespoon baking powder

1/2 teaspoon *each* ground cinnamon and freshly grated nutmeg

1/2 teaspoon salt

Canola-oil spray

1/2 cup (2 oz/60 g) walnuts, toasted and coarsely chopped

Warmed pure maple syrup for serving

Preheat the oven to 200°F (95°C). Pierce the sweet potatoes a few times with a fork, and microwave on high until tender, about 8 minutes. Split each sweet potato lengthwise and let cool just until easy to handle, then scoop out and measure 1¼ cups (6 oz/185 g) of the flesh; reserve the remainder for another use.

In a food processor, combine the warm sweet potato flesh and the butter and pulse until incorporated. Add ½ cup (4 fl oz/125 ml) of the milk, the eggs, brown sugar, and vanilla and process until smooth. Transfer to a bowl and whisk in the remaining 1 cup (8 fl oz/250 ml) milk. In a large bowl, combine the flours, baking powder, cinnamon, nutmeg, and salt. Pour the sweet potato mixture into the flour mixture and stir just until combined. Do not overmix.

Place a griddle over medium heat until hot and coat lightly with canola-oil spray. For each pancake, pour about ¼ cup (2 fl oz/60 ml) of the batter onto the griddle and cook until bubbles break on the surface, about 2½ minutes. Flip the pancakes and cook until golden brown on the second sides, about 2 minutes longer. Transfer to a baking sheet and keep warm in the oven. Repeat with the remaining batter.

Serve the pancakes piping hot, sprinkling each serving with the walnuts. Pass the warmed syrup at the table.

An Apple a Day...

Loaded with antioxidants, apples deserve their reputation for leaving doctors idle. Benefits include reducing the risk of lung cancer and cardiovascular problems. A key substance in apples helps people with asthma. An apple's 5 grams of fiber help to lower bad cholesterol and control weight. An apple's skin holds much of its goodness, but it can be contaminated with pesticides, so consider buying organic.

To preserve their heat-sensitive antioxidants, serve apples raw, or cook them lightly, with the peels if possible. You can also mix shredded apple into your oatmeal and layer it on a nut butter sandwich on whole-grain bread.

Four Ways to Use Apples

Apple & Celery Salad

In a small frying pan, toast 1 teaspoon coriander seeds over medium heat, shaking the pan occasionally, until aromatic, 2–3 minutes. Place in a mortar, crush with a pestle, and set aside. Without peeling them, core and cut 4 tart apples into matchsticks and toss in a bowl with the juice of 1 lemon; 1 teaspoon walnut oil; 2 celery ribs, sliced; the toasted crushed coriander; and salt and pepper to taste. Toss to mix well and serve right away. Serves 4.

Belgian Endive with Apples & Walnuts

In a large bowl, whisk together 1 tablespoon grape seed oil, 1 tablespoon lemon juice, 1 teaspoon toasted walnut oil, and 1 teaspoon grated lemon zest. Quarter 2 Braeburn apples, trim away the core, and cut into very thin wedges. Add the apple wedges, coarsely chopped leaves from 2 heads Belgian endive, and 2 teaspoons chopped fresh tarragon to the bowl and toss to mix well. Sprinkle with ¼ cup (1 oz/30 g) coarsely chopped walnuts and serve right away. Serves 2.

Curried Turkey-Apple Salad

In a large bowl, whisk together 6 tablespoons (3 oz/90 g) plain nonfat yogurt, 2 tablespoons fresh lemon juice, 1 teaspoon honey, 1 teaspoon Madras curry powder, and salt to taste. Add 1½ cups (9 oz/280 g) cubed turkey breast; 1 tart apple, cored and diced; ¼ cup (1½ oz/45 g) minced red onion; and 3 tablespoons toasted chopped almonds. Mix well. Serve in romaine lettuce leaves or on slices of whole-grain bread as a sandwich. Serves 2.

Sautéed Apples

In a large saucepan over medium-high heat, melt 2 tablespoons unsalted butter. Add 1 lb (500 g) tart apples, cored and sliced, and sauté until just tender, 5–7 minutes. Drizzle with 2 tablespoons maple syrup, the juice of ½ lemon, and ½ teaspoon ground cinnamon and stir well. Serves 6.

Scrambling eggs with vegetables and greens is a fast and easy way to prepare a nutritious breakfast. Stir in almost any sautéed vegetables that strike your fancy, such as the tomatoes and zucchini used here. Arugula can stand in for the spinach.

Farmers' Market Scramble

MAKES 4 SERVINGS

8 large eggs

2 tablespoons nonfat milk

Sea salt and freshly ground pepper

4 teaspoons olive oil

1 small zucchini, trimmed and diced

1 ripe medium tomato, seeded and diced

1 cup (1 oz/30 g) firmly packed baby spinach leaves

$1/4$ cup (1 oz/30 g) freshly grated pecorino Romano cheese

In a bowl, whisk together the eggs, milk, and a pinch each of salt and pepper. Continue whisking until the eggs are nice and frothy. Set aside.

Warm the oil in a nonstick frying pan over medium heat. Add the zucchini and another pinch of salt. Cook, stirring, until just tender, about 1 minute. Add the tomato and stir to combine. Reduce the heat to medium-low, add the egg mixture, and let cook, without stirring, until the eggs just begin to set, about 1 minute. Using a heatproof rubber spatula, gently push the eggs around the pan, letting any uncooked egg run onto the bottom of the pan.

When the eggs are about half cooked, 1–2 minutes longer, add the spinach and the cheese. Stir gently to combine and continue cooking until the eggs are completely set but still moist, about another 1 minute.

Transfer the scramble to a warmed platter and serve right away.

Frittatas are another great way to incorporate more vegetables into your diet. They're versatile, easily varied, and can be served warm or at room temperature. To reduce the cholesterol in this recipe, substitute 4 egg whites for 2 of the whole eggs.

Swiss Chard & Onion Frittata

MAKES 4–6 SERVINGS

1 bunch Swiss chard (about 1¼ lb/625 g)

4 tablespoons (2 fl oz/60 ml) olive oil

1 small yellow onion, thinly sliced

Sea salt and freshly ground black pepper

6 large eggs

4 cloves garlic, finely chopped

¼ cup (1 oz/30 g) freshly grated Parmesan cheese

1–2 pinches cayenne pepper

Position a rack in the upper third of the oven and preheat to 350°F (180°C).

Separate the stems from the chard leaves by cutting along both sides of the center vein. Cut the chard stems crosswise into slices ¼ inch (6 mm) thick and coarsely chop the leaves. Set aside separately.

In a large frying pan, heat 2 tablespoons of the olive oil over medium heat. Add the onion and sauté until tender, about 6 minutes. Add the chard stems, season with salt, and sauté until they start to soften, about 4 minutes. Add the chopped chard leaves and sauté until all of the chard is tender, 3–4 minutes longer. Transfer to a plate. Set aside.

In a large bowl, lightly beat the eggs with the garlic and Parmesan. Season with cayenne, salt, and black pepper to taste.

Drain the liquid from the plate holding the chard, squeeze the leaves gently to remove any excess liquid, and stir into the egg mixture. In an 8-inch (20-cm) ovenproof frying pan, heat the remaining 2 tablespoons olive oil over medium-high heat. Add the egg mixture, reduce the heat to medium, and cook without stirring until the eggs are set around the edges, about 5 minutes. Transfer to the oven and bake until completely set, 7–9 minutes longer. Remove from the oven and let cool briefly.

Cut the frittata into wedges and serve straight from the pan, or invert onto a large plate, if desired, cut into wedges, and serve.

Eggs baked in individual ramekins are an easy, cheery breakfast. Just a touch of heavy cream adds silkiness to the dish without too much extra fat. Thick-sliced whole-grain toast is a perfect partner.

Baked Eggs with Spinach

MAKES 4 SERVINGS

Olive-oil cooking spray

1$^1/_3$ cups (3 oz/80 g) coarsely chopped baby spinach

4 extra-large eggs

2 tablespoons heavy cream

Sea salt and freshly ground pepper

Preheat the oven to 375°F (190°C).

Coat the insides of four 6-oz (185-g) ramekins generously with the olive-oil spray. Divide the spinach among the ramekins. Carefully crack an egg into each ramekin over the spinach. Drizzle ½ tablespoon of the cream over each egg and sprinkle with salt and pepper.

Bake until the egg whites are firm and the yolks are cooked to your liking, 10 minutes for soft-set eggs with runny yolks or up to 14 minutes for harder-cooked yolks. Serve right away.

A whole egg baked in a hollowed-out tomato is topped with Parmesan cheese and basil for a novel approach to breakfast. Ripe but firm tomatoes are sturdy enough to hold up to the oven but add lots of sweet juices to the dish.

Eggs Baked in Tomatoes

MAKES 4 SERVINGS

4 medium-size ripe but firm tomatoes

Sea salt and freshly ground pepper

4 large eggs

$^1/_4$ cup (1 oz/30 g) freshly grated Parmesan cheese

1 tablespoon extra-virgin olive oil

$^1/_4$ cup ($^1/_4$ oz/7 g) fresh basil leaves, cut into thin ribbons

Preheat the oven to 450°F (230°C).

Line a rimmed baking sheet with aluminum foil. Using a serrated knife, cut off the top one-fourth of each tomato. Reserve the tomato tops for another use or discard. Using the tip of a spoon, carefully scoop out the insides of the tomatoes, leaving a shell about $^1/_2$ inch (12 mm) thick. Reserve the insides for another use or discard. Place the hollowed-out tomatoes on the prepared baking sheet and sprinkle the insides with a pinch each of salt and pepper.

Carefully crack an egg into each tomato shell and sprinkle 1 tablespoon of the cheese over each egg. Place the baking sheet in the oven and bake until the egg whites are opaque and the yolks have begun to thicken but are still a bit runny, 8–10 minutes.

Remove the egg-filled tomatoes from the oven. Drizzle the tops with olive oil and scatter evenly with the basil. Serve right away.

Pipérade is a Basque-style sauté of sweet onions and colorful peppers. Choose different colors of peppers for the maximum variety of antioxidants, plus a high dose of naturally occurring vitamin C to start your day.

Poached Eggs with Sweet Pepper Pipérade

MAKES 4 SERVINGS

2 tablespoons olive oil

1 small yellow onion, thinly sliced

Sea salt and freshly ground pepper

1 clove garlic, minced

1 *each* red, yellow, and orange bell pepper, seeded and thinly sliced

2 tablespoons white wine vinegar

1 teaspoon sugar

4 large eggs

2 tablespoons chopped fresh flat-leaf parsley

In a frying pan, heat the olive oil over medium heat. Add the onion and a pinch each of salt and pepper. Cook, stirring occasionally, until the onion just begins to soften, 4–5 minutes. Add the garlic and bell peppers and another pinch each of salt and pepper. Cook, stirring occasionally, until the peppers are tender with a bit of a bite and the onion is very soft, 6–8 minutes longer. Stir in 1 tablespoon of the vinegar and the sugar and continue cooking until the vinegar has almost evaporated, 1–2 minutes longer. Cover to keep warm.

Fill a deep sauté pan halfway with cold water. Add 1 teaspoon salt and the remaining 1 tablespoon vinegar and place the pan over medium heat. When the water begins to simmer, break the eggs, one at a time, into a cup and slip each one gently into the water. Cook for 1 minute, then gently slide a spatula under the eggs to prevent sticking. Poach to the desired doneness, 3–5 minutes.

To serve, divide the pepper mixture among individual plates. Using a slotted spoon, scoop the eggs from the simmering water, drain slightly, and place each on top of a serving of peppers. Sprinkle with the parsley and serve right away.

Mexican food can be unhealthy and loaded with fat, although many of its native ingredients, such as beans, tomatoes, and avocados, are considered superfoods. Combined mindfully, as in this dish, they make a healthy south of the border–style breakfast.

Huevos Rancheros

MAKES 4 SERVINGS

4 whole-wheat tortillas

1 tablespoon grapeseed or canola oil, or as needed

4 large eggs

Sea salt and freshly ground pepper

$1^1/_2$ cups (12 fl oz/375 ml) Roasted Tomato Sauce (page 219), warmed in a wide sauté pan

1 cup (8 oz/250 g) fat-free canned refried black beans, warmed

1 small ripe avocado, halved, pitted, peeled, and sliced

$1/_3$ cup ($1^1/_2$ oz/45 g) crumbled feta or cotija cheese

$2/_3$ cup (5 oz/155 g) nonfat plain Greek-style yogurt

1 tablespoon coarsely chopped fresh cilantro

Preheat the oven to 200°F (95°C). Wrap the tortillas in aluminum foil and place in the oven to warm.

In a large frying pan over medium-low heat, warm the oil. Carefully break the eggs into the pan and fry slowly until the whites are set and the yolks have begun to thicken but are not hard, about 3 minutes. Cover the frying pan if you like firm yolks. Season to taste with salt and pepper.

To assemble, remove the tortillas from the oven. Using tongs, dip each tortilla quickly in the warmed tomato sauce and place on warmed individual plates. Spread ¼ cup (2 oz/60 g) of the refried beans evenly on each tortilla and top each with a fried egg. Spoon more of the tomato sauce generously over the eggs and tortilla. Top with the avocado, cheese, yogurt, and cilantro. Serve right away.

Eat Spicy to Improve Your Mood

Capsaicin—the substance that makes chiles burn—stimulates feel-good endorphins in the brain, suppresses appetite, and raises metabolism along with helping to prevent ulcers. Green chiles are rich in vitamin C, ripe red ones in vitamin A. Their ribs contain the heat and transfer it to the seeds, so strip out both (wearing gloves) to reduce a pepper's fire. Chiles have complex flavors ranging from floral to smoky or chocolate.

The heat in chiles is measured in Scoville Heat Units (SHU), starting with 500 SHU for Italian-style pickled pepperoncini and up to 7 million SHU for the meanest hot sauce. The dishes below are medium-hot, but you can add additional hot chiles if you like a spicier kick.

Four Ways to Use Chiles

Pan-Grilled Padrón Peppers

Preheat a stove-top grill pan over high heat until smoking. Meanwhile, in a bowl, toss 1 lb (500 g) padrón peppers with 1 tablespoon olive oil until coated. Place the peppers on the hot grill pan and cook, turning occasionally, until the skin has blistered on all sides, 3–4 minutes. Transfer to a plate, season with flaky sea salt, and serve right away. Serves 4 as an appetizer or snack.

Stuffed Poblano Chiles

Slit 2 poblano chiles and remove the seeds and membranes. Stuff with a mashed mixture of goat cheese, nonfat milk, fresh chives, finely chopped shallots, and salt to taste. Roast the chiles at 400°F (200°C) in a lightly oiled baking dish until soft and slightly wrinkled, 30–40 minutes. Serve right away. Serves 2.

Roasted Chiles & Onions

Cut 8 poblano chiles in half lengthwise and remove the ribs, seeds, and stems. Place the chiles cut side down on a baking sheet and broil, turning as needed, until the skin is blackened all over. Transfer to a heatproof bowl, cover with plastic wrap, and let steam for 5 minutes. Using wet fingers, peel off the blackened skin. Cut the chiles into strips and combine with 1 onion, thinly sliced and sautéed in olive oil. Season with salt and pepper. Serve with egg dishes or as a filling for tacos. Serves 4.

Black Bean & Chile Salad

Roast 2 poblano chiles and cut into strips as directed above in Roasted Chiles & Onions. In a bowl, whisk together ¼ cup (2 fl oz/60 ml) extra-virgin olive oil, 2 tablespoons sherry vinegar, 1 tablespoon Dijon mustard, ½ teaspoon ground cumin, and salt and pepper to taste. Add 2 cans (15 oz/470 g) black beans, rinsed and drained; ½ red onion, minced; 1 pint (370 g) cherry tomatoes, halved; and the pepper strips and toss well. Let stand for a few minutes to blend the flavors. Serves 6.

Rich in vitamin A and beta-carotene from the sweet potatoes and antioxidants from the apples, this is an elegant brunch dish that your guests won't guess is healthful. A small amount of nitrite-free ham adds smoky flavor without too much additional fat.

Sweet Potato Hash with Poached Eggs

MAKES 6 SERVINGS

2 medium-size orange-fleshed sweet potatoes (about 3/4 lb/375 g total weight), peeled and cut into slices 3/4 inch (2 cm) thick

4 teaspoons grapeseed or canola oil

1 cup (5 oz/155 g) finely chopped red onion

1/2 Granny Smith apple, diced

3 oz (90 g) nitrite-free Black Forest ham, diced

2 teaspoons fresh thyme leaves

1/4 teaspoon sweet paprika

1 tablespoon distilled white vinegar

Sea salt

6 large eggs

In a large saucepan fitted with a steamer basket, bring 1 inch (2.5 cm) water to a boil. Put the sweet potato slices in the basket, spread evenly, cover, and steam until the potatoes are tender but still offer some resistance when pierced gently with a fork, about 8 minutes. Remove the pan from the heat, remove the steamer basket from the pan, and let the potatoes cool to room temperature.

In a nonstick frying pan, heat 2 teaspoons of the oil over medium-high heat. Add the onion and apple and sauté until the onion is lightly browned, about 10 minutes. Cut the sweet potatoes into rough cubes and add them to the pan with the ham, thyme, and paprika. Continue to cook, stirring frequently, until the ingredients are browned and warmed through, 5–10 minutes.

While the hash is cooking, poach the eggs: Fill a deep sauté pan halfway with cold water. Add the vinegar and 1 teaspoon salt and place the pan over medium heat. When the water begins to simmer, break the eggs, one at a time, into a cup and slip each one gently into the water. Cook for 1 minute, then gently slide a spatula under the eggs to prevent them from sticking. Poach to the desired doneness, 3–5 minutes.

Divide the hash among individual plates. Using a slotted spoon, scoop the eggs from the simmering water, drain slightly, and place each on top of a serving of hash. Serve right away.

Quesadillas are popular as a lunch dish, but they also make a versatile breakfast. Start with whole-grain tortillas and stuff them with lean chicken breast, scrambled eggs, spinach, tomato, and avocado. They're easy to vary, so you can also make your own healthy combination.

Chicken, Spinach & Avocado Breakfast Quesadillas

MAKES 4 SERVINGS

Olive oil for greasing, plus 1 tablespoon

1 small boneless, skinless chicken breast half (4–5 oz/125–155 g)

Sea salt and freshly ground pepper

4 large eggs

1 cup (2 oz/60 g) coarsely chopped spinach

1 ripe small tomato, seeded and chopped

Two 10-inch (25-cm) whole-wheat tortillas

$1/2$ cup (2 oz/60 g) shredded sharp white Cheddar cheese

$1/4$ cup (2 oz/60 g) nonfat Greek-style yogurt

1 small ripe avocado, pitted, peeled, and sliced

$1/4$ cup (2 oz/60 g) *pico de gallo* (page 218 or purchased)

Preheat the broiler. Lightly oil a broiler pan and set aside.

Place the chicken between 2 pieces of plastic wrap and lightly pound with a meat pounder to a thickness of about $1/2$ inch (12 mm). Brush with oil and season with salt and pepper. Arrange the chicken on the prepared pan and broil, turning once, until lightly browned on both sides and firm when pressed, about 5 minutes total. Transfer to a cutting board and cut into $1/2$-inch (12-mm) dice.

In a bowl, whisk together the eggs, $1/4$ teaspoon salt, and $1/8$ teaspoon pepper. In a frying pan, heat 1 tablespoon olive oil over medium heat. Add the eggs and scramble until starting to set, about 20 seconds. Add the chicken, spinach, and tomato and continue cooking, stirring, until the eggs are just cooked into moist, creamy curds but not dry, about 1 minute. Remove from the heat and set aside.

Warm another frying pan over medium heat. Place 1 tortilla in the hot pan and heat for 1 minute. Flip the tortilla over and sprinkle half of the cheese over the bottom half. Top the cheese with half of the egg-chicken mixture. Fold over the top of the tortilla to cover the filling. Continue cooking until the bottom begins to brown, about 1 minute. Flip and cook until lightly browned on the second side, about 1 minute longer. Transfer to a baking sheet and keep warm in the oven. Repeat to make a second quesadilla.

Cut the quesadillas into wedges. Top each serving with a dollop of yogurt, some avocado slices, and a spoonful of *pico de gallo*. Serve right away.

main dishes

Roasted Tomato & Onion Soup 80

Coconut-Curry Butternut Squash Soup 83

Tuscan-Style Bean & Kale Soup 84

Mushroom & Barley Soup with Fresh Thyme 86

North African–Style Bulgur & Grilled Vegetable Salad 87

Beet & Watercress Salad with Farm Eggs 89

Four Ways to Use Winter Squash 91

Bulgur Salad with Peppers, Chickpeas & Pistachios 93

Quinoa with Tomatoes, Cucumber & Fresh Herbs 94

Whole-Wheat Penne with Spicy Roasted Cauliflower 97

Salmon, Potato & Asparagus Salad 98

Warm Lentil & Kale Salad 101

Four Ways to Use Kale 103

Grilled Salmon with Spicy Melon Salsa 104

Halibut with Roasted Nectarine Chutney 107

Roasted Black Cod with Carrot-Tarragon Purée 108

Sicilian-Style Shrimp with Cauliflower & Almonds 111

Shrimp Tacos with Pineapple Salsa 112

Farro Salad with Turkey, Squash & Dried Cranberries 115

Cashew Chicken Lettuce Tacos 116

Chicken, Broccoli & Mushrooms in Black Bean Sauce 118

Barley Risotto with Chicken, Mushrooms & Greens 119

Four Ways to Use Mushrooms 121

Toasted Quinoa with Chicken & Mango 122

Sautéed Chicken Breasts with Warm Tomato Salad 125

Spicy Ginger Beef & Bok Choy 126

Thai-Style Beef & Herb Salad 129

Steak, Pepper & Onion Salad with Romesco Dressing 130

This simple dish blends three powerful superfoods—tomatoes, garlic, and onions—into a silky soup. The tomatoes are first roasted in a medium-hot oven to concentrate their flavors and enhance their sweetness. Use vegetable broth for a vegetarian version of the soup.

Roasted Tomato & Onion Soup

MAKES 4–6 SERVINGS

3 lb (1.5 kg) ripe tomatoes

2 tablespoons olive oil

2 tablespoons balsamic vinegar

1 clove garlic, minced

2 teaspoons fresh thyme leaves

Sea salt and freshly ground pepper

1 yellow onion, chopped

$1/2$ cup (4 fl oz/125 ml) dry white wine

3 cups (24 fl oz/750 ml) low-sodium chicken broth

2 tablespoons chopped fresh flat-leaf parsley

Preheat the oven to 325°F (165°C).

Cut the tomatoes in half and place, cut side up, on a baking sheet. In a small bowl, whisk together 1 tablespoon of the olive oil, the vinegar, garlic, thyme, $1/4$ teaspoon salt, and $1/4$ teaspoon pepper. Spoon the mixture evenly over the tomatoes. Roast until the tomatoes are soft and wrinkled, about 1 hour.

In a soup pot, heat the remaining 1 tablespoon olive oil over medium-high heat. Add the onion and cook, stirring often and reducing the heat as necessary to prevent scorching, until soft, 5–7 minutes. Add the wine, raise the heat to medium-high, and bring to a boil. Cook until the liquid is evaporated, 2–3 minutes. Stir in the chicken broth and roasted tomatoes, using a wooden spoon to scrape up any browned bits from the bottom of the pan, and return to a boil. Reduce the heat to medium-low, cover, and simmer for 10 minutes to allow the flavors to blend.

In a blender or food processor, working in batches if necessary, process the soup until smooth. Return to the pot and season with salt and pepper. Reheat the soup gently over medium heat just until hot. Ladle into warmed individual bowls, garnish with the parsley, and serve right away.

At once fragrant, sweet, and spicy, this soup is spiked with unexpected Thai flavors. The butternut squash will give the immune system a powerful beta-carotene boost. Garnish it with the leaves and flowers of Thai purple basil leaves, if you like.

Coconut-Curry Butternut Squash Soup

MAKES 4 SERVINGS

1 large butternut squash
(about 4 lb/2 kg)

$1^1/_2$ tablespoons olive oil

4 large shallots, sliced (about 3 oz/90 g)

1 tablespoon peeled and
grated fresh ginger

1 clove garlic, minced

3 cups (24 fl oz/750 ml) low-sodium
chicken or vegetable broth

Sea salt

1 teaspoon Thai red curry paste

$^3/_4$ cup (6 fl oz/180 ml) light coconut milk

2 teaspoons fresh lime juice

Using a sharp, heavy knife, trim the stem end from the squash, then cut in half lengthwise. Scoop out the seeds and discard. Cut off the peel, and then cut the flesh into 1-inch (2.5-cm) cubes. (You should have about 9 cups/3 lb/1.5 kg.)

In a soup pot, heat the olive oil over medium heat. Add the shallots and cook until softened, 2–3 minutes. Add the ginger and garlic and cook until fragrant but not browned, about 1 minute. Add the squash, broth, and ½ teaspoon salt and bring to a boil over high heat. Reduce the heat to maintain a simmer, cover, and cook until the squash is tender when pierced with a fork, about 20 minutes. Remove from the heat and let cool slightly.

In a small bowl, combine the curry paste and coconut milk and whisk until well blended. In a blender or food processor, working in batches if necessary, process the soup until smooth. Return to the pot and stir in the curry–coconut milk mixture. Reheat the soup gently over medium heat just until hot and season with lime juice and additional salt to taste. Ladle into warmed individual bowls and serve right away.

This humble soup is packed with healthy ingredients. The soup holds well and it tastes even better the next day. If you have leftover soup, for a hearty meal, do as the Tuscans do and add stale whole-grain bread to the pot when reheating it.

Tuscan-Style Bean & Kale Soup

MAKES 8 SERVINGS

1 cup (7 oz/220 g) dried borlotti or cranberry beans, soaked and drained

1 bunch Tuscan kale (about ½ lb/250 g)

2 tablespoons olive oil

1 large yellow onion, chopped

1 large carrot, peeled and chopped

1 rib celery, thinly sliced

2 cloves garlic, minced

1 can (28 oz/875 g) whole plum tomatoes

1 bay leaf

Pinch of red pepper flakes

Sea salt and freshly ground black pepper

Pick over the beans for stones or grit. Rinse thoroughly under cold running water and drain. Put the beans in a bowl and add fresh water to cover by 3–4 inches (7.5–10 cm). Let soak for at least 4 hours and up to overnight.

Drain the beans and transfer them to a soup pot. Add water to cover the beans generously. Bring to a boil over high heat, reduce the heat to low, cover partially, and simmer gently until the beans are tender, 1–1½ hours. Drain the beans, pouring their liquid into another pot or a heatproof bowl. Set aside the beans and liquid separately.

Separate the stems from the kale leaves. Stack the leaves, roll them up lengthwise, and cut the leaves crosswise into strips about ½ inch (12 mm) wide. Discard the stems or save them for another use.

In a soup pot, heat the olive oil over medium-high heat. Add the onion, carrot, and celery and sauté until the onion and celery are translucent, 5–7 minutes. Add the kale and stir until wilted, about 5 minutes. Add the garlic and sauté until fragrant, about 1 minute. Pour the tomatoes into a bowl and, using your hands, crush them into small pieces. Add the tomatoes and their juices to the pot and stir to combine.

Measure the bean cooking liquid and add water as needed to total 4 cups (32 fl oz/1 l). Add the beans and the cooking-liquid mixture to the pot along with the bay leaf and red pepper flakes. Bring to a boil over medium-high heat, reduce the heat to medium-low, cover, and simmer just until the beans are heated through, about 10 minutes. Season to taste with salt and black pepper.

Ladle the soup into warmed individual bowls and serve right away.

Dried porcini help to intensify the mushroom flavor in this soup and add an extra savory nuance—umami—to the dish. Simmering barley in a flavorful broth is a pleasing way to get more whole grains in your diet.

Mushroom & Barley Soup with Fresh Thyme

MAKES 4 SERVINGS

$^1/_2$ cup ($^1/_2$ oz/90 g) dried porcini mushrooms

$^1/_2$ cup (4 fl oz/125 ml) dry white wine

1 tablespoon olive oil

2 or 3 large shallots, chopped (about $^1/_2$ cup/2 oz/60 g)

2 cloves garlic, minced

8 oz (250 g) fresh cremini mushrooms, brushed clean and chopped

1 teaspoon minced fresh thyme

Sea salt and freshly ground pepper

3 cups (24 fl oz/750 ml) low-sodium chicken broth

$^3/_4$ cup (5 oz/155 g) pearl barley

1 tablespoon tomato paste

2 teaspoons fresh lemon juice

Rinse the porcini well to remove any dirt or grit. In a small saucepan over medium-high heat, bring the wine to a simmer. Remove from the heat and add the porcini mushrooms. Let stand for 15 minutes. Drain the porcini over a bowl, reserving the liquid, and chop finely.

In a heavy soup pot, heat the olive oil over medium-high heat. Add the shallots and garlic and cook, stirring often, until the shallots are soft, 2–3 minutes. Add the cremini mushrooms, thyme, $^1/_4$ teaspoon salt, and $^1/_4$ teaspoon pepper and sauté until the cremini release their juices and begin to brown, 4–5 minutes. Add the porcini-soaking liquid to the pot and bring to a boil, using a wooden spoon to scrape up any browned bits from the pan. Cook for 1 minute.

Add the chicken broth, barley, tomato paste, chopped porcini, and 3 cups (24 fl oz/750 ml) water to the pot. Bring to a boil, reduce the heat to medium-low, cover, and simmer gently until the barley is tender, 45–50 minutes.

Transfer about 1 cup (8 fl oz/250 ml) of the soup to a blender or food processor and process until smooth. Return the soup to the pot, reheat gently just until hot, and stir in the lemon juice. Taste and adjust the seasoning.

Ladle the soup into warmed individual bowls and serve right away.

This all-purpose grain salad is easy to vary with your favorite grilled vegetables or seasonings. Chickpeas contribute protein and additional fiber and green onions and mint add freshness. For a heartier dish, add grilled chicken breast or salmon.

North African–Style Bulgur & Grilled Vegetable Salad

MAKES 4 SERVINGS

8–10 spears asparagus, trimmed

2 zucchini, cut on the diagonal into slices about 1/4 inch (6 mm) thick

Boiling water as needed

1 teaspoon olive oil

1 1/2 cups (9 oz/280 g) fine-grind bulgur wheat

3 tablespoons extra-virgin olive oil

2 teaspoons finely grated lemon zest

2 tablespoons fresh lemon juice

2 teaspoons ground cumin

1/2 teaspoon ground turmeric

1/2 teaspoon cardamom seeds, crushed

Sea salt and freshly ground pepper

1 cup (7 oz/220 g) drained cooked or canned chickpeas

2 green onions, white and tender green parts, thinly sliced

30 fresh mint leaves, minced

2 tablespoons minced fresh flat-leaf parsley

Prepare a grill for direct-heat cooking over medium heat and oil the grill rack.

Put the asparagus and zucchini in a heatproof bowl, pour over boiling water to cover, and let stand for 2 minutes to soften slightly. Drain, let cool slightly, and toss with the 1 teaspoon olive oil. When the grill is ready, put the bulgur in a heatproof bowl and add boiling water to cover by 2 inches (5 cm). Let stand for 10 minutes. Meanwhile, grill the asparagus and zucchini until lightly browned on all sides and tender-crisp, 4–5 minutes. Transfer to a cutting board and let cool slightly. Cut the asparagus spears on the diagonal into thirds.

In a nonreactive saucepan, whisk together the extra-virgin olive oil, lemon zest and juice, cumin, turmeric, cardamom, 1 teaspoon salt, and several grindings of pepper to make a vinaigrette. Stir in the chickpeas and warm over medium heat for a couple of minutes, stirring occasionally.

Drain the bulgur. Combine the grilled vegetables, bulgur, green onions, mint, parsley, and chickpeas with the vinaigrette in a large serving bowl and toss to coat evenly. Serve warm or at room temperature.

Assertively peppery watercress is a good foil to the sweet, earthy flavor of the beets. Use two colors of beets if you like, or even striped Chioggia beets, if they are available. For the best flavor and vibrant yolk color, seek out eggs from a local egg farm.

Beet & Watercress Salad with Farm Eggs

MAKES 4 SERVINGS

1 1/2–1 3/4 lb (750–875 g) baby beets

6–8 large organic eggs

Sea salt and freshly ground pepper

3 tablespoons extra-virgin olive oil

2 tablespoons Champagne vinegar

2 tablespoons fresh orange juice

1 teaspoon finely grated orange zest

4 oz (125 g) watercress, tough stems removed, torn into bite-size pieces

Preheat the oven to 400°F (200°C).

Trim the root and stem ends from the beets and wrap them in heavy-duty aluminum foil, making a separate packet for each color, if using. Bake until the beets are easily pierced with a sharp knife, 45 minutes–1 hour. Unwrap and let cool. Gently peel the beets with your fingers or a paring knife. Cut into quarters and put in a small bowl.

Place the eggs in a saucepan with enough water to cover by 1 inch (2.5 cm). Bring to a boil over medium-high heat. Remove the pan from the heat, cover, and let stand until done to your liking, about 10 minutes for slightly runny yolks and up to 14 minutes for firm yolks. Drain the eggs, then transfer to a bowl of ice water to cool slightly, 2 minutes or so. Peel the eggs and cut them lengthwise into quarters. Sprinkle each quarter lightly with salt and pepper.

In a large bowl, whisk together the oil, vinegar, orange juice and zest, and 1/2 teaspoon salt to make a dressing. Pour half of the dressing over the beets and stir to coat. In another large bowl, combine the watercress and remaining dressing and toss to coat.

Mound the watercress on individual plates or on a large serving platter and top with the beets. Arrange the egg quarters around the beets and drizzle with any vinaigrette left behind in the watercress bowl. Sprinkle with a few grindings of pepper and serve right away.

Healthy Cold-Weather Staple

Winter squash comes in an assortment of shapes and sizes. Inside their colorful, hard shells, their thick flesh is rich in vitamin A, folate, carotenes, and carotenoids. Many are also good sources of fiber. Their flesh may be dense, fluffy, or wet and stringy, and it may taste nutty, sweet, or somewhat vegetal.

Winter squash is surprisingly versatile. It can star in a warm salad showered with fresh herbs, as a side dish for Thanksgiving, or as a healthy alternative to mashed potatoes. You can also form it into ribbons for a vegetable-based take on a favorite pasta dish.

Four Ways to Use Winter Squash

Warm Squash Salad

Peel 1 small butternut squash and cut into cubes. Toss with 2 tablespoons olive oil and salt and freshly ground pepper to taste and spread on a baking sheet in a single layer. Roast in a 400°F (200°C) oven until tender, 20–30 minutes. In a bowl, whisk together 2 tablespoons extra-virgin olive oil; 2 tablespoons red wine vinegar; 1/2 small red onion, diced; 1 small clove garlic, minced; 1/4 teaspoon red pepper flakes, and salt to taste. Pour the mixture over the squash and toss to coat. Transfer to a platter, sprinkle with 2 tablespoons torn fresh mint leaves, and serve right away. Serves 4.

Maple-Glazed Acorn Squash

Cut 2 small acorn squashes in half lengthwise and scoop out the seeds. Cut the halves crosswise into 1/2-inch (12-mm) slices. Season the slices with salt and pepper and arrange in a single layer on an oiled baking sheet. Roast in a 400°F (200°C) oven for 10 minutes. Meanwhile, in a small saucepan, melt 1 tablespoon butter with 2 tablespoons maple syrup, 1 tablespoon chopped fresh thyme, and 2 teaspoons finely grated orange zest. Brush the squash with the syrup mixture and continue to roast until the slices are tender, 10–15 minutes. Serve right away. Serves 4.

Spaghetti Squash Spaghetti

Cut 1 spaghetti squash (about 4 lb/2 kg) in half lengnthwise, brush with olive oil, and place, cut side down, on a rimmed baking sheet. Roast in a 400°F (200°C) oven until tender, 40–45 minutes. Let cool slightly, then, using a fork, scrape the flesh to remove it in long, spaghetti-like strands. Top with your favorite tomato sauce, warmed; chopped fresh basil; and freshly grated Parmesan cheese. Enjoy it as you would your favorite pasta. Serves 4.

Winter Squash & Pear Purée with Ginger

Roast 1 small butternut squash as directed above in Warm Squash Salad along with 2 peeled, halved, and cored Anjou or Bosc pears until tender. Purée in a food processor along with 1 tablespoon unsalted butter and 1/2-inch piece fresh ginger, peeled and chopped. Reheat if needed before serving. Serves 4.

Roasted peppers and dried fruits add bursts of color and sweetness to this vegetarian supper, while toasted pistachios add crunch. Look for pomegranate molasses in a Middle Eastern grocery or specialty food store.

Bulgur Salad with Peppers, Chickpeas & Pistachios

MAKES 6 SERVINGS

$1^1/_2$ cups (9 oz/280 g) medium-grind bulgur wheat

$2^1/_4$ cups (18 fl oz/560 ml) low-sodium vegetable broth

$^1/_4$ cup (2 fl oz/60 ml) fresh lemon juice

$^1/_4$ cup (2 fl oz/60 ml) pomegranate molasses

2 teaspoons sugar

Sea salt and freshly ground pepper

6 tablespoons (3 fl oz/90 ml) extra-virgin olive oil

1 can ($15^1/_2$ oz/485 g) chickpeas, drained and rinsed

2 large red bell peppers

$^3/_4$ cup (3 oz/90 g) shelled roasted pistachio nuts, toasted

$^1/_2$ cup ($^3/_4$ oz/20 g) chopped fresh flat-leaf parsley or cilantro

1 cup (4 oz/125 g) dried tart cherries, roughly chopped

Put the bulgur in a large heatproof bowl. Bring the broth to a boil in a saucepan, then pour the boiling broth over the bulgur, cover, and let stand until the liquid has been absorbed, about 30 minutes.

In a small nonreactive bowl, whisk together the lemon juice, pomegranate molasses, sugar, $1^1/_2$ teaspoons salt, and several grindings of pepper until the sugar dissolves. Slowly whisk in the olive oil to make a dressing. Adjust the seasoning. In a small bowl, stir together the chickpeas and $^1/_2$ teaspoon salt. Whisk the dressing to recombine, then add it, along with the chickpeas, to the bowl with the bulgur and stir to mix well. Cover and refrigerate for 2 hours.

Preheat the broiler. Place the bell peppers on a small rimmed baking sheet, place under the broiler, and broil, turning occasionally, until the skins are charred on all sides, about 10 minutes. Transfer to a bowl, cover, and let steam for 15 minutes. Remove and discard the skins, stems, and seeds and cut the flesh into small dice.

When ready to serve, in a small bowl, stir together the pistachios and a pinch of salt. Add the pistachios, roasted peppers, parsley, and cherries to the bulgur and toss to mix well. Taste and adjust the seasoning. Divide the salad among individual plates or bowls. Serve right away.

The trio of green onion, parsley, and mint, along with succulent vegetables, brings verdant color and a bold herbal taste to this summery salad. Inspired by traditional Middle Eastern tabbouleh, here protein-rich quinoa stands in for the traditional bulgur.

Quinoa with Tomatoes, Cucumber & Fresh Herbs

MAKES 4 SERVINGS

1 1/2 cups (12 oz/375 g) quinoa

3 cups (24 fl oz/750 ml) low-sodium chicken or vegetable broth

Sea salt and freshly ground pepper

2 large lemons

2 cloves garlic, minced

1 tablespoon pomegranate molasses

1 teaspoon sugar

1/2 cup (4 fl oz/125 ml) extra-virgin olive oil

2 ripe large tomatoes, seeded and diced

1/2 large English cucumber, diced

4 green onions, white and tender green parts, thinly sliced

1/4 cup (1/3 oz/10 g) coarsely chopped fresh flat-leaf parsley

1/4 cup (1/3 oz/10 g) coarsely chopped fresh mint

Put the quinoa in a fine-mesh strainer. Rinse thoroughly under running cold water and drain. In a saucepan, bring the broth to a boil over high heat. Add the quinoa and 1/4 teaspoon salt, stir once, and reduce the heat to low. Cover and cook, without stirring, until all the water has been absorbed and the grains are tender, about 15 minutes. Fluff with a fork and transfer to a large bowl.

Finely grate the zest from 1 of the lemons, then halve both lemons and juice the halves to measure 5 tablespoons (3 fl oz/80 ml). In a small nonreactive bowl, whisk together the lemon juice and zest, garlic, pomegranate molasses, sugar, 1/2 teaspoon salt, and several grindings of pepper until the sugar dissolves. Slowly whisk in the olive oil to make a dressing. Taste and adjust the seasoning. Add about three-fourths of the dressing to the quinoa and stir to mix well.

In a small bowl, toss the tomatoes with 1/4 teaspoon salt and let stand until they release their juice, about 5 minutes, then drain in a sieve set over a second bowl. Place the cucumber in the first bowl along with the green onions and remaining dressing. Toss well, then pour the cucumber mixture over the tomatoes in the sieve to drain. Add the drained tomato-cucumber mixture to the quinoa along with the parsley and mint and stir gently to mix well. Taste, adjust the seasoning, and serve right away.

Roasting cauliflower caramelizes it and brings out its sweetness. Try it in this spicy, Sicilian-style recipe mixed with whole-wheat pasta, capers, and fresh herbs topped with crisp bread crumbs and nutty Parmesan.

Whole-Wheat Penne with Spicy Roasted Cauliflower

MAKES 4–6 SERVINGS

4 slices (each about $^1/_2$ inch/12 mm thick) country-style whole-grain bread

2 cloves garlic, peeled but left whole

2 heads (about 2 lb/1 kg each) cauliflower

3 tablespoons olive oil

Sea salt

$^3/_4$ lb (375 g) whole-wheat penne

$^1/_4$ cup (2 fl oz/60 ml) fresh lemon juice

$^1/_4$ cup ($^1/_3$ oz/10 g) chopped fresh flat-leaf parsley

3 tablespoons capers, drained

1 teaspoon red pepper flakes

$^1/_4$ cup (1 oz/30 g) freshly grated Parmesan cheese

Preheat the oven to 300°F (150°C).

Place the bread slices on a baking sheet and toast until crisp and dry, about 30 minutes. Rub one side of each slice with 1 of the garlic cloves. Let cool, then tear the bread into chunks. Put the chunks in a food processor and process to coarse crumbs. Increase the oven temperature to 400°F (200°C).

Cut each cauliflower into quarters. Discard any leaves and the cores and cut into slices $^1/_4$–$^1/_2$ inch (6–12 mm) thick. Mince the remaining garlic clove. Put the cauliflower in a large baking pan, drizzle with the olive oil, sprinkle with the garlic and $^1/_2$ teaspoon salt, and toss gently to coat evenly. Roast, turning after 10 minutes, until the cauliflower is browned on the edges and tender when pierced with a fork, about 20 minutes.

Meanwhile, bring a large pot three-fourths full of salted water to a boil. Add the pasta to the boiling water and cook until *al dente,* about 12 minutes or according to package directions. Drain, reserving $^1/_2$ cup (4 fl oz/125 ml) of the cooking water. Return the pasta to the pot and add the cauliflower, lemon juice, parsley, capers, red pepper flakes, and reserved cooking water and toss to combine. Stir in the bread crumbs and cheese and serve right away.

This is one of the most heart-healthy salads you can eat. Perfect for a light supper or a lunch, it can be prepared quickly just before serving, or the salmon, potatoes, and asparagus can be prepared up to 1 day ahead, then dressed just before serving.

Salmon, Potato & Asparagus Salad

MAKES 4 SERVINGS

1 lb (500 g) wild salmon fillet

Sea salt and freshly ground pepper

1 lb (500 g) small red-skinned potatoes, scrubbed

³/₄ lb (375 g) asparagus, trimmed and cut into 1-inch (2.5 cm) lengths

10 oz (315 g) mixed baby salad greens (about 8 cups packed)

Sun-Dried Tomato Vinaigrette (page 218)

3 green onions, white and tender green parts, thinly sliced

Preheat the oven to 400°F (200°C).

Season the salmon fillet generously with salt and pepper. Place the salmon in a baking pan and roast until opaque throughout (use a fork to pull apart a flake of flesh and peek), 10–12 minutes. Transfer the salmon to a plate and let cool.

Meanwhile, put the potatoes in a saucepan and add water to cover. Bring to a boil over high heat, reduce the heat to medium-low, cover, and simmer until the potatoes are tender when pierced with a knife, about 15 minutes. Drain and, when cool enough to handle, peel and cut into slices ½ inch (12 mm) thick.

In a large saucepan fitted with a steamer basket, bring 1 inch (2.5 cm) water to a boil. Add the asparagus to the steamer basket, spread evenly, cover, and steam until tender-crisp, about 3 minutes. Remove the steamer basket from the pan and rinse the asparagus under cold running water until cool. Pat dry.

Cut the salmon into 1-inch (2.5-cm) chunks.

In a large bowl, toss the salad greens with 2 tablespoons of the vinaigrette. Add the asparagus and potatoes along with the remaining vinaigrette and green onions and toss gently. Add the salmon pieces and carefully toss just to gently coat. Serve right away at room temperature.

Here, protein- and fiber-rich brown lentils star alongside roasted carrots, sautéed onions, and earthy kale in a salad that shows off bold tastes, textures, and colors. A small amount of crisped prosciutto lends meaty, savory flavor without much extra fat.

Warm Lentil & Kale Salad

MAKES 6 SERVINGS

1 tablespoon olive oil

4 carrots, peeled and diced

1 large red onion, thinly sliced

Sea salt and freshly ground pepper

Leaves from 1 large bunch Tuscan kale, thinly sliced

1 cup (7 oz/220 g) brown lentils, picked over and rinsed

2 sprigs fresh thyme

4 large cloves garlic

4 cups (32 fl oz/1 l) low-sodium chicken broth

6 thin slices prosciutto

1 teaspoon sherry vinegar

In a large saucepan over medium heat, warm the olive oil. Add the carrots and onion, 1/4 teaspoon salt, and several grindings of pepper and sauté until the onion is very soft and lightly caramelized, about 15 minutes. Add the kale leaves to the saucepan, and cook, stirring occasionally, until tender, about 6 minutes. Scrape the contents of the pan into a bowl and set aside. Wipe out the saucepan.

In the same saucepan, combine the lentils, thyme, garlic, chicken broth, 1/2 teaspoon salt, and 1/4 teaspoon pepper and bring to a boil over high heat. Reduce the heat to medium and simmer, uncovered, until the lentils are tender but firm to the bite, 15–20 minutes.

Meanwhile, in a frying pan over medium heat, cook the prosciutto until crisp and browned, about 7 minutes. Let cool, then tear into small pieces.

Drain the lentils in the colander, remove and discard the thyme and garlic, and return the lentils to the saucepan. Stir in the kale mixture, vinegar, and 1/2 teaspoon salt. Taste and adjust the seasoning. Transfer the lentil mixture to a serving bowl. Top with the prosciutto and serve right away.

One of the Healthiest Foods

Among crucifers, kale beats broccoli in
beta-carotene and carotenoid content as well
as in vitamin A and calcium. Ruffle-edged
curly kale is most familiar. Scallop-edged
Russian kale is more tender and milder tasting.
Tuscan kale, also known as *lacinato* kale,
cavolo nero, and dinosaur kale—so-named because
of the bumpy surface of its long, black-green
leaves—can be meltingly tender and mild.

Ideas abound for using the nutritional powerhouse, kale, such as in a nourishing morning smoothie, as a versatile and simple-to-prepare side dish, stirred into a frittata or pasta sauce, or baked to make crisp, satisfying chips to snack on any time of the day.

Four Ways to Use Kale

Green Smoothie

Using a high-speed blender or masticating vegetable juicer, juice 1 bunch washed kale. Blend the juice into your favorite smoothie, ideally made with fruits, for a healthful elixir to start the day. Or, juice the following in a masticating juicer: 1 pear, 1 apple, 1 bunch kale, and ½ cup (¾ oz/20 g) chopped fresh flat-leaf parsley. Add to a blender along with ½ cup (4 oz/125 g) ice cubes and ½ cup (4 fl oz/125 ml) water; whirl until smooth, and serve. Serves 4.

Wilted Garlicky Greens

Remove the stems and tough ribs from 1 bunch kale. Stack the leaves on a cutting board, roll them up lengthwise, then cut them crosswise into thin strips. Wash the leaves well and drain. In a large frying pan over medium-high heat, warm some olive oil and add 1–2 cloves minced garlic and ¼ teaspoon red pepper flakes. Sauté for about a minute, then add the kale and stir to coat. Add a splash of water to the pan, cover, and cook until the greens are tender, about 5 minutes, adding more water if needed. Serves 2–3 as a side dish.

Frittata or Pasta with Greens

Prepare Wilted Garlicky Greens as directed above, then add to your favorite frittata recipe (1 bunch kale is enough for a 6-egg frittata) or add to pasta sauce to enliven your favorite pasta dish (1 bunch kale is sufficient for 12 oz/275 g of dried pasta.)

Smoky Kale Chips

Tear the leaves from the ribs of 1 bunch washed and dried Tuscan kale into fairly large, chip-size pieces, then toss with about 2 tablespoons olive oil, ½ teaspoon Spanish smoked paprika, and about ½ teaspoon salt. Arrange the leaves in a single layer on 1 or more baking sheets and bake in a 300°F (150°C) oven until dry and crisp. Serves 2 as a snack.

Wild salmon is one of the richest sources of omega-3 fats you can find. A versatile fish, it works well with any fruit-based salsa, such as the mixed melon version here. If you like, swap your favorite tropical fruits such as mango or pineapple for the melon.

Grilled Salmon with Spicy Melon Salsa

MAKES 4 SERVINGS

$^1/_2$ cup (3 oz/90 g) *each* finely chopped honeydew, cantaloupe, and watermelon

1 serrano chile, seeded and minced

2 tablespoons coarsely chopped fresh cilantro

1 tablespoon honey

2 teaspoons grated lime zest

1 teaspoon fresh lime juice, or to taste

Salt and freshly ground pepper

$1^1/_2$ lb (750 g) wild salmon fillet, skin removed

Canola oil for greasing, plus 1 tablespoon

In a bowl, stir together the melons, chile, cilantro, honey, lime zest and juice, and a generous pinch each of salt and pepper. Mix well and let stand at room temperature for 15–30 minutes to allow the flavors to blend. Taste and adjust the seasoning with lime juice, salt, and pepper. Set aside.

Prepare a grill for direct-heat cooking over medium-high heat and lightly oil the grill rack. (Alternatively, heat a ridged grill pan on the stove top and brush the pan with oil.)

Sprinkle the salmon all over with salt and pepper, then coat with the 1 tablespoon oil. Arrange the salmon on the grill and cook until nicely grill-marked on the first side, 3–4 minutes. Turn and cook until browned on the second side and done to your liking, 3–4 minutes longer.

Transfer the salmon to a platter and serve right away with the melon salsa.

This method is a little unusual, but useful for a busy cook, as everything is cooked in one pan. Here, vitamin C–packed nectarines are baked to become a fragrant chutney and the fish is roasted right on top.

Halibut with Roasted Nectarine Chutney

MAKES 4 SERVINGS

5 ripe yellow nectarines, halved, pitted, and coarsely chopped

1 tablespoon olive oil, plus more for brushing

$^1/_4$ cup ($1^1/_2$ oz/45 g) golden raisins

2 tablespoons minced red onion

1 teaspoon fresh lemon juice

1 teaspoon light brown sugar

1 teaspoon peeled and grated fresh ginger

4 halibut fillets, about 5 oz (155 g) each

Sea salt and freshly ground pepper

Chopped fresh flat-leaf parsley for garnish

Preheat oven to 400°F (200°C).

In a baking dish, combine the nectarines, 1 tablespoon olive oil, raisins, onion, lemon juice, brown sugar, and ginger. Stir to coat, then spread evenly in the dish.

Brush the fillets with olive oil, then season on both sides with salt and pepper. Place the fillets on top of the nectarine mixture and roast until the fish is opaque throughout and flakes easily with a fork and the fruit is tender, 15–20 minutes.

To serve, place a fillet on each of 4 warmed individual plates, top each with a spoonful of the chutney, and sprinkle with parsley. Serve, passing the remaining chutney at the table.

Roasted fish is always a healthy choice. Black cod is a silky, moist fish that goes with many accompaniments. The vibrant carrot purée, flavored with anise-like tarragon, is a novel, and nutritious, stand-in for mashed potatoes.

Roasted Black Cod with Carrot-Tarragon Purée

MAKES 4 SERVINGS

4 carrots, peeled and cut into 1-inch (2.5-cm) pieces

Sea salt and freshly ground pepper

2 tablespoons low-sodium chicken broth

2 tablespoons low-fat Greek-style yogurt

3 teaspoons minced fresh tarragon

Olive oil for greasing

4 black cod fillets, each about 6 oz (185 g) and 1 inch (2.5 cm) thick

Preheat the oven to 400°F (200°C).

In a saucepan, combine the carrots with water to cover by 1 inch (2.5 cm) and 1 teaspoon salt and bring to a boil over high heat. Cover, reduce the heat to medium, and simmer briskly until the carrots are very tender, 15–20 minutes. Drain the carrots and transfer to a blender or food processor. Add the chicken broth, yogurt, and 1 teaspoon of the tarragon to the blender and process to a smooth purée. Pour back into the saucepan, then taste and adjust the seasoning.

Lightly oil a baking dish just large enough to hold the fish fillets in a single layer. Brush the fillets with olive oil, then season generously on both sides with salt and pepper. Place in the prepared dish and roast until fish is opaque throughout and flakes easily with a fork, 15–20 minutes.

Gently rewarm the carrot-tarragon purée over medium heat, then divide among warmed individual plates and place a fillet on top. Sprinkle with the remaining 2 teaspoons tarragon and serve right away.

Featuring the typical sweet-sour flavors of Sicilian cuisine, nearly every ingredient in this dish is a superfood. For a heartier dish, serve with steamed brown rice or over your favorite whole-wheat pasta shapes.

Sicilian-Style Shrimp with Cauliflower & Almonds

MAKES 4 SERVINGS

$^1/_2$ cup (3 oz/90 g) golden raisins

6 cups (6 oz/185 g) cauliflower florets

2 tablespoons olive oil

$1^1/_2$ yellow onions, chopped

2 cloves garlic, finely chopped

1 cup (6 oz/185 g) chopped ripe yellow or red tomatoes

$^3/_4$ lb (375 g) small shrimp, peeled and deveined

4 anchovy fillets, rinsed and patted dry

$^1/_2$ cup (4 fl oz/125 ml) low-sodium chicken broth

1 teaspoon dried basil

Pinch of red pepper flakes

$^1/_4$ cup (1 oz/30 g) sliced almonds, toasted

Put the raisins in a small bowl and pour over warm water to cover. Let stand until plumped, about 20 minutes.

In a large saucepan fitted with a steamer basket, bring 1 inch (2.5 cm) water to a boil. Add the cauliflower to the steamer basket, spread evenly, cover, and steam until the cauliflower is tender but still offers some resistance when pierced gently with a fork, about 5 minutes. Remove the pan from the heat, remove the steamer basket from the pan, and set aside. Drain the raisins.

In a sauté pan, heat the olive oil over medium-high heat. Add the onions and sauté until lightly browned, 8–10 minutes. Add the garlic and tomatoes and cook, stirring occasionally, until the tomatoes start to break down, about 5 minutes. Add the shrimp and sauté until bright pink, about 3 minutes. Add the anchovies, mashing them with back of a wooden spoon until creamy. Add the cauliflower, raisins, chicken broth, basil, and red pepper flakes. Reduce the heat to medium and cook until the shrimp are opaque throughout, about 3 minutes longer.

Remove from the heat and stir in the almonds. Transfer to a warmed platter and serve right away.

Any color bell pepper will work in this salsa, but for maximum vitamin C and beta carotene, choose red, orange or yellow. If you can't find fresh pineapple, mango or melon could stand in. This recipe can easily be doubled to serve a crowd.

Shrimp Tacos with Pineapple Salsa

MAKES 4 SERVINGS

1 small pineapple (about 2 lb/1 kg), peeled, cored, and diced

$^1/_2$ red onion, finely chopped

$^1/_2$ red bell pepper, seeded and finely chopped

1 small English cucumber, peeled, seeded, and diced

$^1/_2$ jalapeño chile, seeded and finely chopped

$^1/_2$ cup ($^3/_4$ oz/20 g) chopped fresh cilantro

2 tablespoons fresh lime juice

2 tablespoons extra-virgin olive oil

Sea salt and freshly ground pepper

Grapeseed or canola oil for the grill, plus 2 tablespoons

1 lb (500 g) medium shrimp, peeled and deveined

$^1/_2$ teaspoon chipotle chile powder

1 small clove garlic, minced

8 small (6 inches/15 cm) corn tortillas

In a large bowl, combine the pineapple, onion, bell pepper, cucumber, jalapeño, and cilantro and toss to combine. Add the lime juice and olive oil and season with salt and pepper. Stir to mix well. Cover and refrigerate until ready to serve.

Prepare a grill for direct-heat cooking over medium-high heat. Oil the grill rack. Thread the shrimp onto long metal skewers. In a small bowl, mix together the 2 tablespoons grapeseed oil, chile powder, and garlic. Brush the shrimp with some of the oil mixture.

Using tongs, place the shrimp skewers over the hottest part of the fire and grill until bright pink on the first side, about 2 minutes. Turn and cook until bright pink on the second side, about 2 minutes longer. The shrimp should be firm to the touch at the thickest part. Transfer to a plate.

Lightly brush the tortillas with the remaining oil mixture and place over the hottest part of the grill. Grill until they start to puff up, about 1 minute. Using tongs, turn and grill until puffed on the second side, about 1 minute longer.

Place 1 tortilla on each of 4 warmed individual plates. Arrange the shrimp in the center, dividing them evenly, and top each portion with a large spoonful of the salsa. Serve right away, passing the remaining salsa at the table.

In this grain-based salad, sweet-and-sour dried cranberries contrast with cubes of smoked turkey and earthy butternut squash. Nutty farro serves as a backdrop and adds whole-grain goodness to the meal.

Farro Salad with Turkey, Squash & Dried Cranberries

MAKES **6** SERVINGS

$1^1/_3$ cups (8 oz/250 g) semipearled farro

4 cups (32 fl oz/1 l) low-sodium chicken broth

Sea salt and freshly ground pepper

1 small butternut squash (about 2 lb/1 kg)

8 tablespoons (4 fl oz/250 ml) extra-virgin olive oil

$1/_4$ cup (2 fl oz/60 ml) fresh lemon juice

1 teaspoon honey

1 tablespoon minced fresh flat-leaf parsley

6 oz (185 g) boneless smoked turkey, cut into $1/_2$-inch (12-mm) cubes

$2/_3$ cup (3 oz/90 g) sweetened dried cranberries

3 green onions, white and tender green parts, thinly sliced

Pick over the farro for stones or grit. Rinse thoroughly under cold running water and drain. In a saucepan, combine the farro, chicken broth and 1 teaspoon salt and bring to a boil over high heat. Reduce the heat to medium-low and simmer gently, uncovered, until all the liquid has been absorbed and the grains are tender, about 30 minutes. Transfer the farro to a large bowl and let cool to room temperature.

Meanwhile, preheat the oven to 400°F (200°C). Using a sharp, heavy knife, trim the stem end from the squash, then cut in half lengthwise. Scoop out the seeds and discard. Cut off the peel and cut the flesh into $1/_2$-inch (12-mm) cubes. (You should have about $4^1/_2$ cups/$1^1/_2$ lb/750 g.) On a rimmed baking sheet, toss the squash cubes with 2 tablespoons of the olive oil, a generous 1 teaspoon salt, and a generous $1/_4$ teaspoon pepper. Spread the squash cubes in an even layer on the baking sheet and roast until tender but still slightly firm to the bite, about 12 minutes. Let cool.

In a small nonreactive bowl, whisk together the lemon juice, honey, parsley, $1/_4$ teaspoon salt, and several grindings of pepper. Slowly whisk in the remaining 6 tablespoons (3 fl oz/90 ml) olive oil to make a dressing. Adjust the seasoning.

Add the dressing, squash, turkey, cranberries, and green onions to the cooled farro and toss to mix well. Serve right away.

This playful spin on tacos starts with a savory Asian-style chicken-and-vegetable stir-fry, then uses crisp, fresh romaine lettuce as a stand-in for tortillas. Chopped cashew nuts add healthy crunch and fresh cilantro adds freshness.

Cashew Chicken Lettuce Tacos

MAKES 4 SERVINGS

2 heads romaine lettuce hearts

$1/4$ cup (2 fl oz/60 ml) low-sodium chicken broth

2 tablespoons hoisin sauce

1 tablespoon low-sodium soy sauce

1 teaspoon rice vinegar

$1/4$ teaspoon Asian sesame oil

1 tablespoon cornstarch

2 tablespoons grapeseed or canola oil

$3/4$ lb (375 g) boneless, skinless chicken breasts, cut into $1/2$-inch (12-mm) cubes

3 cloves garlic, minced

1 medium green bell pepper, seeded and diced

1 large red bell pepper, seeded and diced

4 green onions, white and tender green parts, sliced

1 jalapeño chile, thinly sliced

$1/2$ cup (2 oz/60 g) coarsely chopped raw cashews

Roughly chopped cilantro (optional)

Using your fingers, separate the lettuce leaves from the lettuce heads, tearing out any tough ribs and discarding any blemished or discolored leaves. Place the leaves on a plate, cover with moist paper towels, and refrigerate.

In a small bowl, whisk together the chicken broth, hoisin sauce, soy sauce, vinegar, sesame oil, and cornstarch. Set aside.

In a wok or a large nonstick frying pan, heat the grape seed oil over medium-high heat until almost smoking. Add the chicken and stir-fry until browned, 1–2 minutes. Using a slotted spoon, transfer the chicken to a plate. Add the garlic, bell peppers, green onions, and jalapeño and stir-fry until tender-crisp, about 2 minutes. Return the chicken to the pan and add the cashews. Whisk the soy sauce mixture to recombine, add to the pan, and stir-fry until the chicken is opaque throughout and the sauce is nicely thickened, 2–3 minutes longer.

Scrape the contents of the pan onto a warmed platter. Serve right away with the lettuce leaves. Instruct diners to spoon the chicken-vegetable mixture into the lettuce leaves, add cilantro, if desired, fold them up like tacos, and eat.

Stir-frying calls for cooking foods quickly over high heat in a small amount of fat, which is a healthy choice. Prep all the ingredients for this one—packed with vitamins and lean protein—ahead of time, as the cooking goes quickly.

Chicken, Broccoli & Mushrooms in Black Bean Sauce

MAKES 4 SERVINGS

1 tablespoon fermented black beans

4 tablespoons dry sherry

1/2 lb (250 g) ground chicken breast

1 teaspoon Asian sesame oil

Sea salt and ground white pepper

2 tablespoons grapeseed or canola oil

6 cloves garlic, chopped

1 tablespoon peeled and grated fresh ginger

2 cups (4 oz/125 g) broccoli florets

2 cups (6 oz/185 g) sliced cremini mushrooms

2 or 3 large shallots, chopped (about 1/2 cup/2 oz/60 g)

2 tablespoons low-sodium chicken broth

Steamed brown rice for serving

1/4 cup (1/3 oz/10 g) fresh Thai basil leaves, torn

In a small bowl, soak the black beans in 2 tablespoons of the sherry for 20 minutes. Drain, discarding the sherry.

In a medium bowl, combine the chicken with the sesame oil, 1/2 teaspoon salt, and 1/8 teaspoon white pepper and stir to coat mix well. Cover with plastic wrap and let stand at room temperature for 20 minutes.

In a wok or a large nonstick frying pan, heat the grapeseed oil over medium-high heat until almost smoking. Add the chicken mixture and stir-fry, breaking up the meat with a spatula until no pink remains, about 2 minutes. Using a slotted spoon, transfer the chicken to a plate. Add the garlic, ginger, and black beans and stir-fry until fragrant, about 30 seconds. Add the broccoli, mushrooms, and shallots and stir-fry until the vegetables begin to soften, about 2 minutes. Add the chicken broth and remaining 2 tablespoons sherry and stir to combine. Return the chicken to pan and stir-fry until the pan is almost dry, 2–3 minutes longer.

To serve, spoon the rice into warmed individual bowls or onto a warmed platter and top with the chicken and vegetables, dividing them evenly. Garnish with the basil and serve right away.

Barley has a pleasantly chewy texture and a sweet, nutty flavor. When simmered in broth over low heat, it cooks into a creamy risotto-style dish. Add meaty mushrooms, shredded chicken, and peppery arugula and you have a delicious fall dinner.

Barley Risotto with Chicken, Mushrooms & Greens

MAKES 6 SERVINGS

6 cups (48 fl oz/1.5 l) low-sodium chicken broth

1¹/₂ tablespoons olive oil

1 yellow onion, chopped

1 clove garlic, minced

2 cups (6 oz/185 g) sliced cremini mushrooms

Sea salt and freshly ground pepper

¹/₂ cup (4 fl oz/125 ml) dry white wine

1 cup (7 oz/220 g) pearl barley

3 cups (4 oz/125 g) firmly packed baby arugula

2 cups (12 oz/375 g) diced or shredded cooked chicken

¹/₂ cup (2 oz/60 g) freshly grated Parmesan cheese

In a saucepan over medium-high heat, bring the chicken broth to a boil. Remove from the heat and cover to keep warm.

In a large saucepan, heat the olive oil over medium-high heat. Add the onion and cook, stirring often, until soft, about 5 minutes. Add the garlic and cook until fragrant, about 1 minute. Add the mushrooms, ¹/₄ teaspoon salt, and a few grindings of pepper. Cook, stirring often, until the mushrooms release their juices and start to brown, 4–5 minutes. Add the wine, bring to a boil, and simmer for 1 minute.

Add 5 cups (40 fl oz/1.25 l) of the hot broth and the barley. Cover and simmer over medium-low heat, stirring occasionally and adding more broth ¹/₄ cup (2 fl oz/60 ml) at a time if barley becomes dry, until the barley is tender, about 45 minutes. Stir in the arugula and more broth to loosen the mixture a little, if needed. Cook, uncovered, until the greens are wilted, about 2 minutes. Stir in the chicken and cook for 1 minute to heat through. Stir in the Parmesan and season to taste with additional salt and pepper. Serve right away.

A Magical Source of Nutrients

The health benefits of mushrooms, particularly shiitakes and wild maitakes, seem almost miraculous. They contain substances unique to mushrooms and so effective that in Asia they are used medicinally to help boost the body's immune system. Even cultivated white button mushrooms, brown cremini, and Portobello mushrooms are rich in anti-cancer selenium and other minerals. They provide good quality protein, as well.

With a pleasing texture and naturally savory flavor, mushrooms make a great snack either on their own topped with pesto, or as a topping for grilled bread. When roasted, they also make a novel side dish or hearty topping for a salad of healthy greens and herbs.

Four Ways to Use Mushrooms

Mushroom Bruschetta

In a small bowl, stir together 3 tablespoons olive oil, 2 tablespoons fresh lemon juice, 1 crushed garlic clove, and salt and pepper to taste. Add 1 lb (500 g) portobello mushroom caps and turn to coat. Brush 8 slices country-style whole-grain bread with olive oil and cook on a medium-hot grill or grill pan until lightly grill-marked, about 1 minute per side. Grill the mushrooms until softened and browned, about 3 minutes per side, then slice and arrange slices on the grilled bread. Sprinkle with chopped fresh basil and shaved Parmesan cheese and serve right away. Serves 4.

Pesto Portobellos

Sprinkle 8 portobello mushrooms caps with lemon juice, salt, and pepper. Cook the mushrooms, gill side down, over a medium-hot grill or grill pan until browned, about 3 minutes. Turn over the mushrooms so they are gill side up, spoon on a little pesto (page 218 or purchased) and cook until the mushrooms are soft and the pesto bubbles, 3–5 minutes. Serve right away. Serves 4.

Garlicky Mushrooms with Pine Nuts

In a bowl, toss 1 lb (500 g) assorted mushrooms with ¼ cup (2 fl oz/60 ml) olive oil, 4 chopped garlic cloves, and salt and pepper to taste. Spread in a roasting pan in a single layer and pour over 2 tablespoons dry white wine or broth. Roast in a 450°F (230°C) oven until they begin to sizzle and brown, about 15 minutes. Add ⅓ cup (2 oz/60 g) pine nuts and continue to roast until tender and browned, about 10 minutes longer. Sprinkle with chopped fresh herbs and serve right away. Serves 4.

Roasted Mushroom Salad

Follow the recipe for Garlicky Mushrooms above, omitting the pine nuts and herbs. Make a dressing from 5 tablespoons (3 fl oz/80 ml) extra-virgin olive oil, ½ teaspoon chopped fresh thyme, ¼ cup (2 fl oz/60 ml) balsamic vinegar, 1 teaspoon fresh lemon juice, a drop of agave nectar, and salt and pepper to taste. In a large bowl, toss together 1 head torn radicchio, 1 small head torn red-leaf lettuce, 1 cup (1½ oz/45 g) fresh flat-leaf parsley, and salt and pepper to taste. Toss with the dressing according to your taste. Divide among plates and top each serving with the warm mushrooms. Serves 6.

This protein-packed dish is simple to make. Its mango-cucumber-yogurt raita features flavors influenced by the cooking of India. You can also serve the raita with grilled or roasted fish or pork.

Toasted Quinoa with Chicken & Mango

MAKES 4 SERVINGS

²/₃ cup (5 oz/155 g) quinoa

3 tablespoons low-fat plain yogurt

1 tablespoon fresh lemon juice

1 teaspoon peeled and grated fresh ginger

1 teaspoon honey

Sea salt and freshly ground pepper

2 cups (10 oz/315 g) diced mango

³/₄ cup (4 oz/125 g) seeded and sliced cucumber

4 boneless, skinless chicken breast halves, about 6 oz (185 g) each

1 tablespoon grapeseed or canola oil

Torn fresh mint for garnish

Put the quinoa in a fine-mesh strainer. Rinse thoroughly under running cold water and drain. Transfer the wet quinoa to a dry nonstick sauté pan and place over medium heat. Toast the quinoa, stirring constantly, with a wooden spatula, until the grains are dry, 2–3 minutes. Raise the heat to medium-high and continue stirring until the grains start popping and the quinoa is lightly browned, about 6 minutes. Remove from the heat and pour in 2 cups (16 fl oz/500 ml) water; be careful, as it will splatter. Return to medium-high heat, cover, and bring to a boil, then reduce the heat to medium-low and simmer gently until tender, about 15 minutes.

Meanwhile, in a bowl, whisk together the yogurt, lemon juice, ginger, honey, and ¼ teaspoon salt. Add the mango and cucumber and stir to coat evenly. Set aside.

One at a time, place the chicken breasts between 2 pieces of plastic wrap and lightly pound with a meat pounder to a thickness of about ½ inch (12 mm). Season the chicken generously on both sides with salt and pepper.

In a large nonstick frying pan, heat the oil over medium-high heat. Working in batches if necessary to avoid crowding the pan, add the chicken and reduce the heat to medium. Cook, turning once, until nicely browned and opaque throughout, 4–5 minutes per side. Transfer each piece to a plate as it is finished and cover with aluminum foil to keep warm.

To serve, fluff the quinoa with a fork and divide among 4 warmed dinner plates. Slice the chicken and place it on top of the quinoa. Top with the mango-yogurt mixture and mint and serve right away.

Cherry tomatoes, which pack a healthful punch, are often seen as a garnish and left behind on the plate. Here, as a sauté atop lean chicken breasts, they make a nutritious, one-dish weeknight supper.

Sautéed Chicken Breasts with Warm Tomato Salad

MAKES 4 SERVINGS

4 boneless, skinless chicken breast halves, about 6 oz (185 g) each

Sea salt and freshly ground pepper

2 tablespoons olive oil

1 or 2 large shallots, minced (about ¼ cup/1 oz/30 g)

1 clove garlic, minced

1½ cups (9 oz/280 g) cherry and pear tomatoes, preferably a mix of colors and shapes, stemmed and halved

3 tablespoons balsamic vinegar

½ cup (½ oz/15 g) packed fresh basil leaves, torn

One at a time, place the chicken breasts between 2 pieces of plastic wrap and lightly pound with a meat pounder to a thickness of about ½ inch (12 mm). Season the chicken generously on both sides with salt and pepper.

In a large nonstick frying pan, heat the olive oil over medium-high heat. Working in batches if necessary to avoid crowding the pan, add the chicken and reduce the heat to medium. Cook, turning once, until nicely browned and opaque throughout, 4–5 minutes per side. Transfer each piece to a plate as it is finished and cover with aluminum foil to keep warm.

Add the shallots and garlic to the frying pan and cook, stirring often, until softened, 3–4 minutes. Add the tomatoes and vinegar and cook, still stirring often, until the tomatoes begin to soften and split, about 4 minutes. Stir in the basil and season with salt and pepper.

To serve, place a chicken breast on each of 4 warmed individual plates and spoon the warm tomato salad on top. Serve right away.

Lean flank steak is easier to slice if you chill it in the freezer for about 30 minutes. Serve this quick stir-fry with steamed brown rice. If you like, add color and more nutrients to the dish by stir-frying red onions and red bell peppers along with the bok choy.

Spicy Ginger Beef & Bok Choy

MAKES 4 SERVINGS

2 tablespoons dry sherry

1 tablespoon low-sodium soy sauce

$1/2$ teaspoon Asian red chile paste, plus more if desired

1 lb (500 g) baby bok choy

1 tablespoon grapeseed or canola oil

2 cloves garlic, minced

1 tablespoon peeled and minced fresh ginger

1 lb (500 g) flank steak, thinly sliced across the grain

In a small bowl, stir together the sherry, soy sauce, and chile paste. Set aside.

Trim the stem ends from the baby bok choy and separate into leaves.

In a wok or a large nonstick frying pan, heat $1/2$ tablespoon of the oil over high heat. When the oil is hot, add the bok choy and cook, stirring, just until tender-crisp, about 2 minutes. Transfer to a bowl.

Add the remaining $1/2$ tablespoon oil to pan. When hot, add the garlic and ginger and cook, stirring often, until fragrant but not browned, about 30 seconds. Add the beef to the pan and cook, tossing and stirring, just until no longer pink, about 2 minutes.

Return the bok choy to the pan along with the sherry mixture and cook for 1 minute until heated through. If you like your food extra spicy, top with additional red chile paste. Serve right away.

This salad contains an abundance of vegetables and fresh herbs that are high in beta-carotene and other protective phytochemicals. Tossed with lean steak and a low-fat vinaigrette featuring Thai flavors, it is reminiscent of salads typical of Southeast Asia.

Thai-Style Beef & Herb Salad

MAKES 4 SERVINGS

3 tablespoons Thai fish sauce

3 tablespoons fresh lime juice

2 teaspoons sugar

1–2 teaspoons minced fresh hot chiles with seeds

Grapeseed or canola oil for greasing, plus 2 teaspoons

1 small flank steak ($3/4$–1 lb/375–500 g)

Sea salt and freshly ground pepper

1 large head butter or other soft-textured leaf lettuce, torn into bite-sized pieces

1 cup (5 oz/155 g) thinly sliced English cucumber

$1/2$ cup ($1^3/4$ oz/50 g) thinly sliced red onion

$1/2$ cup ($2^1/2$ oz/75 g) red bell pepper strips

$1/2$ cup ($3/4$ oz/20 g) lightly packed torn fresh mint leaves

$1/2$ cup ($3/4$ oz/20 g) lightly packed torn fresh cilantro leaves

$1/4$ cup ($1/3$ oz/10 g) lightly packed torn fresh basil leaves, preferably Thai

In a large bowl, stir together the fish sauce, lime juice, sugar, and chiles to make a vinaigrette. Set aside.

Prepare a charcoal or gas grill for direct-heat cooking over high heat, or preheat the broiler. Oil the grill rack. Sprinkle the flank steak evenly with salt and pepper and rub them into the meat. Brush lightly on both sides with the 2 teaspoons oil.

Place the flank steak directly over the heat and grill, turning once, until seared on the outside and cooked rare to medium-rare in the center, about 4 minutes per side. (Alternatively, place the flank steak on a broiler pan and slip it under the broiler about 2 inches/5 cm from the heat source. Broil, turning once, until the meat is seared on the outside and cooked rare to medium-rare in the center, about 4 minutes per side.)

Transfer the steak to a cutting board, tent with aluminum foil, and let rest for 20 minutes.

Cut the steak across the grain on the diagonal into very thin slices. Add the slices to the vinaigrette and toss to coat. Add the lettuce, cucumber, onion, bell pepper, mint, cilantro, and basil and toss to coat. Serve right away.

This salad is a riot of garden-fresh color, which also means it is deeply nutritious. Smoked paprika lends intensity and appealing red color to a steak marinade and romesco-style dressing and echoes the charred flavors from the grill.

Steak, Pepper & Onion Salad with Romesco Dressing

MAKES 6 SERVINGS

6 tablespoons (2 fl oz/60 ml) extra-virgin olive oil

$1/3$ cup (3 fl oz/80 ml) sherry vinegar

2 tablespoons fresh orange juice

1 tablespoon Spanish smoked paprika

5 cloves garlic, minced

$1^1/2$ tablespoons fresh oregano leaves

$1^3/4$–2 lb (875 g–1 kg) flank steak

2 small red onions, cut into thick slices

3 red, yellow, or orange bell peppers, seeded and cut into wide strips

Sea salt and freshly ground pepper

$1/2$ large head green leaf lettuce, leaves torn into bite-sized pieces

Romesco Dressing (page 218)

2 tablespoons chopped fresh flat-leaf parsley

In a glass dish large enough to hold the steak, whisk together $1/4$ cup (2 fl oz/ 60 ml) of the olive oil, the vinegar, orange juice, paprika, garlic, and oregano until well blended. Lay the steak in the dish and turn a few times to coat it evenly. Cover and refrigerate for at least 2 hours and preferably overnight, turning once or twice. Let come to room temperature before grilling.

Prepare a grill for direct-heat cooking over medium-high heat. Oil the grill rack.

Brush the onions and peppers with the remaining 2 tablespoons olive oil and season with salt and pepper. Grill, turning once, until softened and lightly charred on both sides, 7–10 minutes for the onions and about 15 minutes for the peppers. Transfer to a plate. Remove the meat from the marinade (discard the marinade) and season both sides with salt and pepper. Grill, turning once, until browned on both sides and cooked to your liking, 10–15 minutes. Transfer to a cutting board and tent with aluminum foil. Cut the peppers into $1/2$-inch (12 mm) strips and separate the onion slices into rings.

In a bowl, toss the lettuce with $1/8$ teaspoon salt. Divide the lettuce evenly among individual plates. Cut the steak across the grain on the diagonal into thin slices. Top each mound of lettuce with an equal amount of the steak, onion, and peppers. Spoon the dressing over each salad, dividing evenly, and sprinkle each with a little parsley. Serve right away.

sides & snacks

Grilling bitter radicchio caramelizes and sweetens the leaves. Salsa verde adds piquancy and colorful contrast. Be sure to taste the salsa before seasoning, as its anchovies and capers both have natural saltiness.

Pan-Grilled Radicchio with Salsa Verde

MAKES 4 SERVINGS

4 heads treviso radicchio (about 1¼ lb/125 g total weight)

Extra-virgin olive oil for drizzling, plus 8 tablespoons (4 fl oz/125 ml)

Sea salt and freshly ground pepper

1 lemon

2 cloves garlic, smashed

2 tablespoons capers

1 teaspoon prepared horseradish

2 olive oil–packed anchovy fillets, preferably Italian

Leaves from 1 bunch fresh flat-leaf parsley

Leaves from ½ bunch fresh mint

Remove and discard any blemished or discolored leaves from the radicchio heads, then cut each head lengthwise into quarters. Put the quarters on a baking sheet, drizzle them lightly with olive oil, sprinkle lightly with salt and pepper, and toss to coat. Set aside.

Finely grate the zest from the lemon, then halve it and squeeze the juice from one half into a small bowl. Set aside the remaining half.

In a food processor, combine the lemon zest, garlic, capers, horseradish, and anchovies. Process until well chopped. Add the parsley and mint leaves, lemon juice, and 2 tablespoons of the olive oil. Pulse until the mixture forms a coarse purée. With the motor running, slowly pour in the remaining 6 tablespoons (3 fl oz/90 ml) olive oil and process until smooth; the salsa should have the consistency of pesto. Transfer the mixture to a bowl and taste and adjust the seasoning. If desired, add a bit more lemon juice or water to loosen the sauce.

Heat a ridged grill pan on the stove top over medium heat. When the pan is hot, add the radicchio quarters in a single layer and cook until they just begin to wilt and caramelize, 2–3 minutes per side. Transfer to a serving plate and drizzle with the salsa verde. Serve hot or at room temperature.

This trio of chunky vegetables, fresh herbs, and protein-rich quinoa makes a balanced side dish for any meal. It is also a perfect meatless dinner. A small amount of feta cheese adds tanginess and additional protein.

Yellow Squash & Red Quinoa Salad

MAKES 6 SERVINGS

1 1/2 cups (8 oz/250 g) red quinoa

2 tablespoons plus 1/4 cup (2 fl oz/60 ml) extra-virgin olive oil

1 lb (500 g) yellow crookneck squash, cut into 1/2-inch (12-mm) chunks

Sea salt

1 clove garlic

1/4 cup (2 fl oz/60 ml) fresh lemon juice

1 small cucumber, cut into 1/2-inch (12-mm) chunks

5 green onions, white and tender green parts, cut on the diagonal into 1/4-inch (6-mm) pieces

1/4 cup (1/3 oz/10 g) chopped fresh basil

1/4 cup (1/3 oz/10 g) chopped fresh mint

1/2 cup (2 1/2 oz/75 g) crumbled feta cheese

Put the quinoa in a fine-mesh strainer. Rinse thoroughly under running cold water and drain. In a saucepan, bring 3 cups (24 fl oz/750 ml) water to a boil over high heat. Add the quinoa, stir once, and reduce the heat to low. Cover and cook, without stirring, until all the water has been absorbed and the grains are tender, about 25 minutes. Let it stand for a few minutes, covered, then fluff with a fork and transfer to a large bowl.

Meanwhile, in a large frying pan, heat the 2 tablespoons olive oil over medium-high heat. Add the squash, season with salt, and cook, stirring often, until tender-crisp, 3–4 minutes. Transfer to a plate and let cool.

On a cutting board, using a fork or the flat side of a chef's knife, mash the garlic into a paste with a pinch of salt. In a small bowl, stir together the mashed garlic and lemon juice and let stand for 10 minutes. Whisk in the 1/4 cup (2 fl oz/60 ml) olive oil to make a vinaigrette.

Put the quinoa, squash, cucumber, green onions, basil, mint, and feta in a large bowl. Drizzle with the vinaigrette and toss gently to mix and coat well. Taste and adjust the seasoning. Serve right away.

The deeper green color of leafy greens like broccoli rabe, kale, and chard indicate that they contain higher amounts of vitamins and other nutrients than the lighter greens used in salads. Here is an all-purpose recipe that can be used for any type of dark green.

Spicy Broccoli Rabe with Garlic

MAKES 4–6 SERVINGS

Sea salt

1 lb (500 g) broccoli rabe, trimmed

1 tablespoon olive oil

3 cloves garlic, thinly sliced

$^1/_4$ teaspoon red pepper flakes

1 tablespoon fresh lemon juice

Bring a large saucepan two-thirds full of salted water to a boil over high heat. Add the broccoli rabe and cook until just tender, about 4 minutes. Drain well.

In a large frying pan, heat the olive oil over medium-high heat. Add the garlic and red pepper flakes and cook, stirring constantly, until the garlic is fragrant but not browned, about 30 seconds. Add the broccoli rabe and ½ teaspoon salt. Stir to coat the broccoli rabe with the seasoned oil and cook just until warmed through, 1–2 minutes. Remove from the heat and stir in the lemon juice.

Transfer to a warmed platter and serve right away.

In this dish, fragrant toasted walnut oil and tart wine vinegar counter the bitterness of the brussels sprouts. Toasted walnuts contribute another layer of warm nuttiness and a crunchy texture.

Sweet & Sour Brussels Sprouts with Walnuts

MAKES 4 SERVINGS

1 lb (500 g) brussels sprouts

1 tablespoon olive oil

Sea salt and freshly ground pepper

1 cup (8 fl oz/250 ml) low-sodium chicken broth

2 tablespoons red wine vinegar

1 tablespoon light brown sugar

2 teaspoons roasted walnut oil

$1/4$ cup (1 oz/30 g) walnut pieces, toasted

Using a small, sharp knife, trim the bases of the brussels sprouts. Remove and discard any blemished or discolored leaves.

In a large frying pan, heat the olive oil over medium heat. Add the brussels sprouts, spread in a single layer, and sprinkle lightly with salt. Cook, stirring once or twice, until the sprouts are golden brown and caramelized on all sides, about 4 minutes.

Raise the heat to medium-high and add the chicken broth. Bring the broth to a boil and, using a wooden spoon, scrape up any browned bits from the bottom of the pan. Reduce the heat to medium-low, cover partially, and simmer until most of the liquid has evaporated and the sprouts are just tender when pierced with a knife, about 20 minutes.

Add $1/4$ cup (2 fl oz/60 ml) water to the pan, stir in the vinegar and brown sugar, and raise the heat to medium-high. Cook, stirring occasionally, until the liquid reduces and thickens to a glaze, 2–3 minutes. Remove the pan from the heat and stir in the walnut oil and walnut pieces. Taste and adjust the seasoning with salt and pepper.

Transfer to a warmed serving bowl and serve right away.

Eating cabbage regularly can significantly lower your risk of cancer and this recipe shows a great way to do it. Green apples bring sweetness and bright flavor, red wine adds depth, and a sprinkle of orange zest contributes freshness to this hearty side dish.

Balsamic-Braised Red Cabbage with Apples

MAKES 4–6 SERVINGS

3 tablespoons olive oil

1 yellow onion, thinly sliced

Sea salt and freshly ground pepper

1 tablespoon honey

1 Granny Smith apple, halved, cored, and thinly sliced

$1/4$ cup (2 fl oz/60 ml) balsamic vinegar

1 cup (8 fl oz/250 ml) dry red wine

1 head red cabbage (about 2 lb/1 kg), cored and cut into thin shreds

Finely grated zest of 1 orange

In a large frying pan, heat the olive oil over medium heat. Add the onion and a pinch of salt and sauté until the onion is soft and translucent, 5–7 minutes. Add the honey and cook for 1 minute longer. Add the apple slices and vinegar, raise the heat to medium-high, and use a wooden spoon to scrape up any browned bits from the bottom of the pan. Bring the liquid to a boil, then add the wine and 1 cup (8 fl oz/250 ml) water. Season with a generous pinch each of salt and pepper and return to a boil. Reduce the heat to medium-low and simmer until the liquid begins to reduce, about 10 minutes.

Add the cabbage. Using tongs, toss to coat well with the liquid in the pan. Cover the pan and cook, stirring occasionally, until the cabbage begins to wilt, 25–30 minutes. Uncover and cook until the cabbage is tender and most of the liquid has evaporated, 25–30 minutes longer.

Taste and adjust the seasoning. Remove the pan from the heat and stir in the orange zest, then transfer the cabbage to a warmed bowl and serve right away.

With its savory blend of mustard, garlic, and smoky bacon, this recipe will turn even the most finicky eater into a brussels sprout fan. The bacon is added sparingly–just a half slice per serving–to give complexity and flavor with just a little fat.

Warm Brussels Sprouts Salad

MAKES 6 SERVINGS

2 tablespoons red wine vinegar

$^1/_2$ teaspoon grainy mustard

1 clove garlic, minced

$^1/_4$ cup (2 fl oz/60 ml) extra-virgin olive oil

Sea salt and freshly ground pepper

$1^1/_2$ lb (750 g) brussels sprouts

3 slices bacon, cooked until crisp and finely crumbled

In a small bowl, whisk together the vinegar, mustard, and garlic. Whisking constantly, pour in the olive oil in a slow, steady stream to make a vinaigrette. Season with salt and pepper and set aside.

Using a small, sharp knife, trim the bases of the brussels sprouts. Remove and discard any blemished or discolored leaves. Separate the leaves of the sprouts, continuing to use the knife to cut away the cores.

In a large saucepan over medium heat, combine the brussels sprout leaves and ½ cup (4 fl oz/125 ml) water. Cover, raise the heat to high, and bring to a boil. Reduce the heat to medium-low and cook until the leaves are bright green and tender, about 7 minutes, adding more water if needed. Drain thoroughly and transfer to a warmed serving bowl.

Drizzle the vinaigrette over the brussels sprouts and toss to coat. Taste and adjust the seasoning. Sprinkle with the bacon and serve right away.

Any color of beet can be used here, but keep in mind that red beets can color your fingers. To avoid stains, wear rubber gloves when peeling them. Chioggia beets, with their concentric red and white rings, bleed only slightly, and golden beets not at all.

Beet, Orange & Fennel Salad

MAKES 4 SERVINGS

4 red or golden beets
(about 1 lb/500 g total weight)

2 teaspoons olive oil

2 oranges

1 fennel bulb

2 tablespoons orange-infused olive oil

1 teaspoon red wine vinegar

1 teaspoon balsamic vinegar

Sea salt and freshly ground pepper

$^1/_2$ cup (2 oz/60 g) freshly grated pecorino Romano cheese

$^1/_4$ cup (1 oz/30 g) slivered almonds, toasted

Position a rack in the middle of the oven and preheat to 350°F (180°C).

Place the beets in a single layer in a shallow baking dish. Drizzle with the olive oil and rub to coat. Roast, turning occasionally, until the beets are easily pierced with a sharp knife and the skins are slightly wrinkled, about 1¼ hours. Remove from the oven and let cool. When cool enough to handle, cut off the stems and remove the skins with your fingers. Cut each beet into quarters.

Cut a thick slice off the top and bottom of each orange. Working with 1 orange at a time, stand it upright and, following the contour of the fruit, carefully slice downward to remove the peel, pith, and membrane. Holding the orange over a bowl, cut along each section of the membrane, letting each freed section drop into the bowl. Strain the oranges, reserving 2 teaspoons of the juice.

Cut off the stems and feathery leaves from the fennel bulb and set aside. Discard the outer layer of the bulb if it is tough. Quarter the bulb lengthwise and cut off the core and any tough base portions. Cut the fennel lengthwise into slices about ¼ inch (6 mm) thick. Add to the bowl. Add the beets to the bowl with the reserved orange juice, the orange-infused olive oil, the red wine and balsamic vinegars, ½ teaspoon salt, and ¼ teaspoon pepper. Toss gently to coat and mix well.

Divide the salad among individual plates. Chop the fennel fronds. Sprinkle the salad with the cheese, toasted almonds, and fennel fronds and serve right away.

Good for Bone Health

Broccolini is a cross between broccoli and *gai lan*, a Chinese vegetable. Sweeter and milder than broccoli (page 8) it offers as much vitamin C as orange juice. It also provides a substantial amount of folate, vitamin A and potassium, as well as some iron, calcium, vitamin B and fiber.

Broccoli and broccolini make great side dishes when roasted or steamed and can be seasoned with a wide variety of flavorings influenced by cuisines around the globe. Added to pasta, they bring substance and nutrition to an easy main dish.

Four Ways to Use Broccoli & Broccolini

Roasted Broccoli with Mustard & Pine Nuts

In a large roasting pan, toss 2 lb (1 kg) broccoli florets, with 2 tablespoons olive oil. Spread in the pan in a single layer, then roast in a 400°F (200°C) oven until browned and tender, stirring once or twice, 20–30 minutes. In a bowl, whisk together 2 tablespoons balsamic vinegar, 1 teaspoon grainy mustard, and 1 tablespoon olive oil. Pour over the broccoli and toss well. Sprinkle with ¼ cup (1 oz/30 g) toasted pine nuts and serve right away. Serves 6.

Broccolini with Soy-Sesame Vinaigrette

In a large bowl, whisk together 1 tablespoon toasted sesame oil, 1 tablespoon low-sodium soy sauce, 2 teaspoons fresh lemon juice, and 1 drop dark agave nectar. Steam 1½ lb (750 g) broccolini until tender-crisp, 7–10 minutes. Add the warm broccolini to the soy mixture and toss well to coat. Sprinkle with 2 teaspoons toasted sesame seeds and serve right away. Serves 4.

Broccoli or Broccolini with Orange & Almonds

Toss 1½ lb (750 g) broccoli florets or trimmed broccolini with 1½ tablespoons olive oil and spread in a roasting pan in a single layer. Roast in a 425°F (220°C) oven until browned, about 25 minutes. Transfer to a serving dish and drizzle with 1 tablespoon fresh orange juice, 1 teaspoon grated orange zest, and 2 tablespoons chopped toasted almonds. Serves 4.

Pasta with Broccoli, Garlic & Anchovies

In a large frying pan over medium heat, sauté 6 finely chopped anchovy fillets and 5 cloves thinly sliced garlic in ¼ cup (2 fl oz/60 ml) olive oil until the garlic is lightly golden, 1–2 minutes. Add 1 lb (500 g) blanched broccoli florets, a pinch of red pepper flakes, and salt to taste and sauté for 2–3 minutes to heat through. Add ¼ cup (2 fl oz/60 ml) dry white wine and cook until nearly evaporated, 1–2 minutes. Toss with 1 lb (500 g) cooked whole-wheat pasta and serve topped with freshly grated Parmesan cheese. Serves 4–6.

This quick dish pairs tender asparagus with meaty shiitake mushrooms for a satisfying vegetable stir-fry. Sesame seeds are densely nutritious and offer a surprising array of health benefits, including cholesterol-lowering potential.

Stir-fried Asparagus with Shiitakes & Sesame Seeds

MAKES 4–6 SERVINGS

1 lb (500 g) asparagus, tough ends snapped off

3 tablespoons canola or grapeseed oil

1 clove garlic, minced

1 tablespoon peeled and grated fresh ginger

6 oz (185 g) shiitake mushrooms, stems removed, caps brushed clean and thinly sliced

$1/4$ cup (2 fl oz/60 ml) dry white wine or sake

$1/4$ cup (2 fl oz/60 ml) low-sodium chicken broth

$1^1/2$ tablespoons low-sodium soy sauce

2 teaspoons sesame seeds

Cut the asparagus on the diagonal into 2-inch (5-cm) pieces.

In a large frying pan, heat the oil over high heat. Add the garlic and ginger and cook, stirring constantly, until fragrant but not browned, about 30 seconds. Add the mushrooms and cook, stirring often, until they begin to brown, about 2 minutes. Add the asparagus and cook, stirring constantly, until bright green and tender-crisp, about 3 minutes.

Stir in the wine, broth, and soy sauce and cook until the liquid is reduced to a saucelike consistency and all the vegetables are tender, 2–3 minutes longer. Stir in the sesame seeds, transfer to a warmed serving dish, and serve right away.

Of the many types of sweet potatoes, the dark orange-fleshed ones are an especially healthful choice because they are high in fiber and beta-carotene. In this simple recipe, the seasoned potatoes are garnished with antioxidant-rich fresh cilantro.

Roasted Sweet Potatoes with Cumin & Cilantro

MAKES 4 SERVINGS

2 orange-fleshed sweet potatoes (about 1 lb/500 g total weight), peeled

1 tablespoon canola or grapeseed oil

1 teaspoon ground cumin

Sea salt and freshly ground pepper

2 tablespoons finely chopped fresh cilantro

Preheat the oven to 400°F (200°C).

Cut the sweet potatoes crosswise into rounds ½ inch (12 mm) thick. Rinse the slices under cold running water and spread on a clean kitchen towel; blot dry with a second kitchen towel.

Put the sweet potatoes in a bowl. Drizzle with the oil, sprinkle with the cumin, and toss to coat evenly.

Preheat a nonstick baking sheet in the oven for 5 minutes. Remove from the oven and carefully arrange the sweet potatoes in a single layer on the hot baking sheet. Roast the sweet potatoes, turning every 10 minutes, until evenly browned and tender when pierced with a knife, 30–35 minutes.

Transfer the sweet potatoes to a warmed serving dish and sprinkle with ½ teaspoon salt, a grinding or two of pepper, and the cilantro. Toss gently to coat. Serve right away.

Cauliflower is an excellent source of potassium and vitamin C and has cancer-fighting properties. Soaking cauliflower before baking is an important step. Advise each diner to squeeze on a little lemon juice at the table.

Cauliflower with Orange Zest & Green Onion

MAKES 4 SERVINGS

1 head cauliflower (about 1³/₄ lb/875 g), cored and cut into uniform-sized florets

1 tablespoon olive oil

Sea salt and freshly ground pepper

2 tablespoons coarsely chopped green onion

2 tablespoons chopped fresh flat-leaf parsley

2 teaspoons grated orange zest

4 lemon wedges

Put the cauliflower florets in a large bowl and add cold water to cover. Let stand for 20–30 minutes, then drain and pat dry.

Preheat the oven to 400°F (200°C).

Spread the cauliflower in a single layer in a 9-by-13-inch (23-by-33-cm) baking dish. Drizzle with the olive oil, sprinkle with salt and pepper, and toss to coat. Roast, turning every 10 minutes and sprinkling with 1–2 tablespoons cold water each time, until the florets are tender and lightly browned, about 30 minutes.

Pile the green onion, parsley, and orange zest on a cutting board and finely chop them together. Using your fingers, toss the finished mixture on the board to distribute all the ingredients evenly. When the cauliflower is done, remove it from the oven and sprinkle evenly with the green-onion mixture. Spoon the cauliflower into a warmed serving dish and garnish with the lemon wedges. Serve right away.

A trio of spices commonly found in curry blends of India lend an exotic flavor to earthy-sweet roasted beets. If your beets come with tops, cut them off and then save them for sautéeing as you would Swiss chard or kale.

Indian-Spiced Roasted Beets

MAKES 4 SERVINGS

1 teaspoon ground cumin

1 teaspoon ground coriander

$1/2$ teaspoon ground turmeric

Sea salt and freshly ground pepper

6 red beets (about $1^3/4$ lb/875 g total weight)

2 tablespoons canola or grapeseed oil

Fresh cilantro leaves for garnish

Preheat the oven to 350°F (180°C).

In a small bowl, combine the cumin, coriander, turmeric, 1 teaspoon salt, and 1 teaspoon pepper and stir to mix well.

If the beet greens are still attached, cut them off, leaving $1/2$ inch (12 mm) of the stems attached. (Save the greens for another use.) Arrange the beets in a shallow baking dish just large enough to hold them in a single layer. Drizzle with the oil and turn to coat, then rub with the spice mixture, coating the beets evenly. Roast, turning occasionally, until the beets are easily pierced with a sharp knife and the skins are slightly wrinkled, about $1^1/4$ hours. Remove from the oven and let cool. When cool enough to handle, cut off the stems and remove the skins with your fingers.

Cut each beet lengthwise into wedges, sprinkle with cilantro, and serve warm or at room temperature.

This is an unusual way to prepare broccolini: a half lemon is cut, peel and all, and roasted with the vegetables. The other seasonings are minimal—just garlic, salt, and pepper—for a suprisingly complex flavor from just six ingredients.

Roasted Broccolini with Lemon

MAKES 4 SERVINGS

2 lb (1kg) broccolini, trimmed and coarsely chopped

$1/2$ lemon

$1^1/2$ tablespoons olive oil

2 cloves garlic, minced

Sea salt and freshly ground pepper

Preheat the oven to 350°F (180°C).

Trim and coarsely chop the broccolini. Remove the seeds from the lemon and then cut it, peel and all, into $1/4$-inch (6-mm) dice.

In a frying pan, heat 1 tablespoon of the olive oil over medium-high heat. Add the garlic and cook, stirring constantly, until lightly golden, about 1 minute. Add the broccolini, diced lemon, $1/2$ teaspoon salt, and a few grindings of pepper. Cook, stirring often, just until color of the broccolini deepens, about 1 minute longer.

Scrape the contents of the frying pan into a baking dish, add the remaining $1/2$ tablespoon olive oil, and turn to coat. Roast until the broccolini is tender-crisp, 10–12 minutes. Transfer to a platter and serve warm or at room temperature.

Cooking the cauliflower in a smoking-hot pan until well browned brings out its natural sweetness. This dark, caramel-like flavor is enhanced by the spicy glaze and a splash of tart, vitamin C–rich lemon juice.

Sweet & Smoky Caramelized Cauliflower

MAKES 4 SERVINGS

2 tablespoons unsalted butter

3 tablespoons olive oil

1 large head cauliflower (about 3 lb/ 1.5 kg), cored and cut into 1-inch (2.5-cm) florets

Sea salt and freshly ground black pepper

1 shallot, minced

$1/2$ teaspoon smoked sweet paprika

$1/4$ teaspoon red pepper flakes

2 tablespoons honey

$1/2$ lemon

In a large frying pan over medium heat, melt the butter with 2 tablespoons of the olive oil. Add the cauliflower florets, sprinkle with a generous pinch of salt, and toss gently to coat the florets with the seasoned oil. Spread the florets in a single layer in the pan and cook, without stirring, until lightly browned on the bottom, 3–4 minutes. Using tongs, turn each piece and continue cooking, undisturbed, until evenly browned on the second side, 3–4 minutes. Repeat until all sides are evenly browned, 3–5 minutes longer.

Add the remaining 1 tablespoon olive oil, the shallot, paprika, and red pepper flakes to the pan. Cook, stirring occasionally, until the shallot is softened, 1–2 minutes. Add the honey and 2 tablespoons water and sauté until the liquid reduces to a glaze, 2–3 minutes. Squeeze the juice from the lemon half over the cauliflower, stir to combine, and cook just to warm through, about 30 seconds. Remove from the heat. Taste and adjust the seasoning with salt and black pepper.

Transfer the cauliflower to a warmed serving bowl and serve right away.

Traditionally, ratatouille is a dish of summer vegetables that are simmered for a long time in their own juices. In this version, the vegetables are cut into large pieces and roasted briefly, which concentrates and intensifies their flavors.

Roasted Ratatouille

MAKES 6–8 SERVINGS

1 lb (500 g) plum tomatoes, halved lengthwise

4 large cloves garlic, sliced

1 large yellow onion, halved and cut crosswise into slices $1/4$ inch (6 mm) thick

1 small eggplant, trimmed and cut into 1-inch (2.5-cm) chunks

1 small zucchini, trimmed and cut crosswise into slices $1/2$ inch (12 mm) thick

1 small yellow crookneck squash, trimmed and cut crosswise into slices $1/2$ inch (12 mm) thick

1 green bell pepper, seeded and cut into $1^1/_2$-inch (4-cm) squares

5 tablespoons (3 fl oz/80 ml) olive oil

Sea salt and freshly ground pepper

$1/4$ cup ($1/_3$ oz/10 g) finely shredded fresh basil

2 tablespoons chopped fresh thyme

Preheat the oven to 425°F (220°C).

Combine the tomatoes, garlic, onion, eggplant, zucchini, yellow squash, and bell pepper in a large bowl. Drizzle in the olive oil, sprinkle generously with salt, and toss to coat. Transfer the vegetables to a large rimmed baking sheet and spread in an even single layer.

Roast the vegetables, stirring once or twice, for 20 minutes. Remove from the oven and sprinkle with the basil and thyme. Continue to roast, again stirring once or twice, until the biggest pieces are tender when pierced with a fork, 5–10 minutes longer. Remove the vegetables from the oven and season with salt and pepper.

Transfer the ratatouille to a bowl. Serve hot, warm, or at room temperature.

The Redder the Better

Tomatoes are rich in vitamins A and C, carotenes and carotenoids. As they redden, their carotenoid content increases. Refrigerating retards this, destroys flavor, and turns them mushy, so keep tomatoes on a shady counter. When they are in season, from summer through fall, eat locally grown vine-ripe tomatoes, particularly heirloom varieties in every color available. Since you eat the skins, buying organic is best.

Tomatoes are abundant at the market during summer and early fall. Since they are such nutritional powerhouses, use them often. Cooking tomatoes makes lycopene, a powerful antioxidant, easier for the body to use.

Four Ways to Use Tomatoes

Roasted Tomatoes

Cut 3 lb (1.5 kg) heirloom tomatoes in half and place, cut side up, on a baking sheet. In a small bowl, mix together 1 tablespoon olive oil, 2 tablespoons balsamic vinegar, 1 minced garlic clove, ¼ teaspoon *each* salt and freshly ground pepper, and the leaves from 1 sprig fresh thyme. Spoon the mixture evenly over the tomatoes and bake in a 325°F (165°C) oven until the tomatoes are soft and wrinkled, about 1 hour. Add to pastas, vegetable dishes, sandwiches, and pizzas. Makes about 2 cups (16 oz/500 g).

White Beans with Tomatoes & Basil

In a bowl, mix together 2 cans (15 oz/470 g) each white kidney (cannellini) beans, rinsed and drained; 2 tomatoes, seeded and chopped; ¼ cup finely chopped red onion; 2 tablespoons balsamic vinegar; 1 tablespoon extra-virgin olive oil; 3 tablespoons torn fresh basil leaves, and salt and pepper to taste. Let stand for 30 minutes or refrigerate for up to 4 hours before serving. Serves 4.

Tomato Pesto

Place ½ cup (1½ oz/45 g) dry-packed sun-dried tomatoes in a heatproof bowl, add boiling water to cover, and let stand for 15 minutes to re-hydrate. Drain the tomatoes, then add to a food processor along with 2 plum tomatoes, diced; ½ cup (¾ oz/20 g) packed fresh basil leaves; 1 chopped garlic clove; and ½ teaspoon salt and process until puréed. With the motor running, slowly drizzle in 2 tablespoons extra-virgin olive oil until blended. Use on pizzas, or with pastas or vegetables. Makes about 1 cup (8 oz/250 g).

Heirloom Tomatoes with Sherry Vinaigrette

In a small bowl, whisk together 3 tablespoons extra-virgin olive oil, 1 tablespoon sherry vinegar, 1 minced large shallot, and salt and pepper to taste. Core 1–1½ lb (500–750 g) heirloom tomatoes, preferably in different colors, and cut into thin wedges. Arrange on a platter, drizzle with the vinaigrette, and serve sprinkled with your favorite chopped fresh herbs. Serves 4.

Low-calorie spaghetti squash is a great stand-in for pasta and its long strands take to sauces just as well. This simple side dish is sprinkled with cheese and fresh herbs, but you could also toss the squash with your favorite tomato sauce.

Spaghetti Squash with Garlic, Oregano & Parmesan

MAKES 4 SERVINGS

1 spaghetti squash (about 2 lb/1 kg)

1 tablespoon extra-virgin olive oil

1 small clove garlic, minced

Sea salt and freshly ground pepper

$^{1}/_{4}$ cup (1 oz/30 g) finely grated Parmesan cheese

1 teaspoon minced fresh oregano

Preheat the oven to 350°F (180°C).

Using a sharp, heavy knife or a cleaver, trim the stem end from the squash, then cut it in half lengthwise. Scoop out the seeds and discard. Place the halves, cut side down, in a baking dish and add $^{1}/_{3}$ cup (3 fl oz/80 ml) water. Bake until tender, about 1 hour.

Transfer the squash to a cutting board. When cool enough to handle, use a fork to scrape out flesh in noodlelike strands, scraping all the way to skin. Place the squash in a serving bowl and add the olive oil, garlic, $^{1}/_{2}$ teaspoon salt, and $^{1}/_{2}$ teaspoon pepper. Stir gently to mix well. Sprinkle with the Parmesan and toss to combine. Taste and adjust the seasoning. Sprinkle with the oregano and serve right away.

Yellow tomatoes have a sweeter, less acidic flavor than red tomatoes, but red ones can be substituted for the yellow here, or use equal amounts of each. If using red tomatoes, reduce the amount of red wine vinegar slightly.

Green Bean & Yellow Tomato Salad with Mint

MAKES 4 SERVINGS

1 lb (500 g) long, slender green beans

$^1/_2$ cup ($^3/_4$ oz/20 g) chopped fresh mint

2 tablespoons extra-virgin olive oil

Sea salt and freshly ground pepper

1 or 2 ripe yellow tomatoes

$^1/_2$ cup (2 oz/60 g) thin red onion wedges

2 teaspoons red wine vinegar, or to taste

Bring a large saucepan two-thirds full of water to a boil over high heat. Trim the ends of the beans. Add the beans to the boiling water and cook until tender, 5–7 minutes; the timing will depend on their size. Drain thoroughly and pat dry.

In a large serving bowl, combine the hot green beans, mint, olive oil, and $^1/_2$ teaspoon salt and toss to mix. Set aside and let cool to room temperature, about 20 minutes.

Cut the tomatoes into wedges about $^1/_2$ inch (12 mm) thick. Just before serving, add the tomatoes, onion, 2 teaspoons vinegar, and a grind of pepper to the bean mixture and toss to mix. Taste and add more vinegar or salt and pepper, as needed. Serve at room temperature.

A small amount of prosciutto or lean bacon used in a dish lends complexity without adding a lot of extra fat. It's a good strategy to use when cooking bland-tasting legumes, such as the lentils here.

Lentils with Shallots & Prosciutto

MAKES 4 SERVINGS

³/₄ cup (5 oz/155 g) brown lentils

1 tablespoon olive oil

³/₄ cup (4 oz/125 g) finely chopped fresh fennel bulb

¹/₄ cup (1 oz/30 g) finely chopped shallots

2 tablespoons sherry vinegar

2 oz (60 g) prosciutto, cut into ribbons

Sea salt and freshly ground pepper

Chopped fresh fennel fronds for garnish

Pick over the lentils for stones or grit. Rinse thoroughly under cold running water and drain. In a saucepan, combine the lentils with water to cover by 2 inches (5 cm) and bring to a boil over medium-high heat. Reduce the heat to medium-low, cover, and simmer gently until the lentils are tender but firm to the bite, about 20 minutes. Scoop out ¹/₄ cup (2 fl oz/ 60 ml) of the cooking liquid and reserve. Drain the lentils thoroughly in a colander, then return to the saucepan.

In a frying pan, heat the olive oil over medium-high heat. Add the fennel and shallots and cook, stirring often, until golden, about 8 minutes. Scrape the contents of the frying pan into the saucepan with the lentils. Add the vinegar and reserved lentil-cooking liquid to the frying pan, bring to a boil, and cook until the liquid is reduced by half, about 3 minutes. Add the hot liquid to the lentils and stir in the prosciutto. Season to taste with salt and pepper.

Transfer the lentils to a serving bowl or platter, sprinkle with the fennel fronds, and serve right away.

A speedy sauté brings out the natural sweetness and enhances the crunch of two kinds of spring peas. Anise-like fresh basil, tart lemon zest, and tangy pecorino cheese are sprinkled on top for a delicious, fresh and fast side dish.

Sautéed Garden Peas with Basil & Pecorino

MAKES 4 SERVINGS

1 tablespoon unsalted butter

1 tablespoon olive oil

$^1/_2$ lb (250 g) sugar snap peas, strings removed

1 lb (500 g) English peas, shelled

Sea salt and freshly ground pepper

1 lemon

Leaves from 4 fresh basil sprigs, torn

About 1 oz (30 g) chunk pecorino Romano cheese

In a large frying pan over medium heat, melt the butter with the olive oil. Add the sugar snap peas and English peas. Pour in $^1/_4$ cup (2 fl oz/60 ml) water and add a pinch of salt. Cover and cook for 2 minutes. Uncover and cook, stirring occasionally, until the water has evaporated, about 2 minutes longer. The peas should be tender-crisp and still bright green.

Finely grate 2 teaspoons zest from the lemon, then halve the lemon. Remove the pan from the heat and squeeze the juice from 1 lemon half over the peas (reserve the remaining half for another use). Add the lemon zest, basil, and a pinch each of salt and pepper to the pan. Grate cheese over the top to taste and stir to mix well.

Transfer the peas to a warmed serving dish and serve right away.

Large pieces of winter squash can take a long time to cook, but when sliced thinly, it cooks in about 15 minutes. This means you can take advantage of squash's dense nutrition even on a weeknight, as in this dish that also stars sweet pears and fragrant rosemary.

Butternut Squash & Pears with Rosemary

MAKES 4 SERVINGS

1 Bosc pear

1 tablespoon grapeseed or canola oil

$^1/_2$ small butternut squash (about $^3/_4$ lb/ 375 g), peeled, seeded, and thinly sliced

Sea salt

1 tablespoon finely chopped fresh rosemary

Pinch of cayenne pepper

$^1/_2$ cup (4 fl oz/125 ml) apple juice

Halve and core the pear and cut it lengthwise into thin slices.

In a frying pan, heat the oil over medium-high heat. Add the squash and sprinkle with 1 teaspoon salt. Cook, stirring often, until the squash is browned on the edges and begins to soften, about 5 minutes.

Add the pear, rosemary, cayenne, and apple juice and cook until the liquid evaporates and the squash is tender, 6–8 minutes longer.

Transfer to a serving bowl. Serve hot, warm, or at room temperature.

Medium-grain brown rice has a sticky texture and nutlike aroma and taste. A whole grain with its bran intact, it is far more healthful than white rice. Sesame seeds enhance the rice's nutty flavor and contribute calcium.

Sesame Brown Rice

MAKES 4 SERVINGS

1 cup (7 oz/220 g) medium-grain brown rice

Sea salt

2 teaspoons sesame seeds

1 teaspoon Asian sesame oil

1 tablespoon thinly sliced green onion tops

In a saucepan, bring 2¾ cups (22 fl oz/680 ml) water to a boil over high heat. Add the rice and ½ teaspoon salt, stir once, and reduce the heat to low. Cover and simmer very gently, without stirring, until all the water has been absorbed and the grains are tender, 35–45 minutes.

Meanwhile, in a small, dry frying pan over medium heat, toast the sesame seeds, stirring constantly, until they are fragrant and have darkened slightly, about 2 minutes. Immediately pour the seeds onto a plate to cool. Set aside.

Carefully lift the cover of the saucepan so that no condensation drips into the rice. Drizzle the sesame oil evenly over the top and sprinkle with half of the sesame seeds. Gently fluff the rice with a fork or the handle of a wooden spoon.

Spoon the rice into a warmed serving dish. Sprinkle with the remaining sesame seeds and the green onion. Serve right away.

Whole grain bulgur and easy-to-cook lentils combine with aromatic vegetables, fragrant spices, and fresh herbs in a versatile pilaf to accompany any meal. A topping of toasted almonds lends protein and crunch.

Bulgur & Lentil Pilaf with Almonds

MAKES 4 SERVINGS

$^3/_4$ cup (5 oz/155 g) brown lentils

2 tablespoons olive oil

1 yellow onion, chopped

2 cloves garlic, minced

1 cup (6 oz/185 g) medium-grain bulgur wheat

1 teaspoon ground coriander

Sea salt and freshly ground pepper

2 cups (16 fl oz/500 ml) low-sodium vegetable broth or water

$^1/_4$ cup (1$^1/_2$ oz/45 g) roasted almonds

$^1/_3$ cup ($^1/_3$ oz/10 g) fresh flat-leaf parsley leaves

1 tablespoon grated lemon zest

2 tablespoons fresh lemon juice

Pick over the lentils for stones or grit. Rinse thoroughly under cold running water and drain. In a small saucepan, combine the lentils with water to cover by 2 inches (5 cm) and bring to a boil over medium-high heat. Reduce the heat to medium-low, cover, and simmer gently until tender but firm to the bite, about 20 minutes. Drain thoroughly and set aside.

In a large frying pan, heat the olive oil over medium-high heat. Add the onion and cook, stirring often, until the onion is wilted, 2–3 minutes. Add the garlic, bulgur, coriander, $^1/_4$ teaspoon salt, and $^1/_4$ teaspoon pepper and cook, stirring often, until the garlic is fragrant, about 1 minute. Stir in the lentils and the broth and bring to a boil. Reduce the heat to low, cover, and simmer for 5 minutes. Remove from the heat and let stand, covered, for 15 minutes.

Place the almonds, parsley, and lemon zest on a cutting board and coarsely chop them together. Fluff the pilaf with a fork and stir in the lemon juice. Season to taste with salt and pepper. Mound the pilaf on a serving platter, sprinkle with the almond mixture, and serve right away.

When shopping for farro, look for "semipearled," or "semiperlato," which means that it has been partially polished to remove some of its hull. It will cook more quickly, but still retain some whole-grain benefits.

Farro Salad with Artichoke Hearts

MAKES 4–6 SERVINGS

1¹/₄ cups (10 oz/315 g) semipearled farro

Sea salt and freshly ground pepper

¹/₂ cup (2¹/₂ oz/75 g) pine nuts

¹/₄ cup (1¹/₂ oz/45 g) olive oil–packed sun-dried tomatoes

1 jar (14 oz/440 g) artichoke hearts (not marinated)

6 tablespoons (3 fl oz/90 ml) red wine vinegar

3 tablespoons extra-virgin olive oil

¹/₂ cup (2¹/₂ oz/75 g) finely chopped red onion, rinsed and thoroughly drained

¹/₂ cup (³/₄ oz/20 g) chopped fresh flat-leaf parsley

Pick over the farro for stones or grit. Rinse thoroughly under cold running water and drain. In a saucepan, combine the farro, 2¹/₂ cups (20 fl oz/625 ml) water and a generous pinch of salt and bring to a boil over high heat. Reduce the heat to medium-low, cover, and simmer gently until all the water has been absorbed and the grains are tender, 25–30 minutes.

In a small, dry frying pan over medium heat, toast the pine nuts, stirring often, just until fragrant and lightly browned, 2–3 minutes. Be careful not to let them burn. Immediately pour onto a plate to cool. Set aside.

Drain the sun-dried tomatoes, reserving the oil to use in place of some of the olive oil, if you like. Cut the tomatoes into julienne. Drain the artichokes, rinse, and drain again. Cut into quarters.

In a large bowl, whisk together the vinegar and olive oil (or a mixture of the tomato oil and olive oil, if using). Add the farro, tomatoes, artichoke hearts, onion, parsley, and pine nuts and toss gently to mix and coat well. Season generously with salt and pepper. Serve right away.

Give Your Liver a Boost

Eating an artichoke down to its meaty heart takes patience, but it's worth it when you consider it offers good and unique, rarely found, liver-detoxifying compounds. To better preserve their antioxidants and vitamin C, choose steaming over boiling artichokes. An alternative is paring the vegetable while raw and discarding the fuzzy choke to expose its meaty heart and then using it in a variety of dishes.

Serve artichokes Italian-style—thinly sliced raw in a salad. Braising or steaming are other healthy options. So is buying artichoke hearts in a jar or frozen to make Farro Salad with Artichoke Hearts (page 177). (Just make sure they are not sulfite-treated.)

Four Ways to Use Artichokes

Shaved Artichoke Salad

Halve 8 medium artichokes lengthwise and using a small spoon, remove the fuzzy choke. As the artichokes are trimmed, immerse them in lemon water. Slice the artichokes thinly lengthwise, put them in a bowl, and toss with 2 tablespoons extra-virgin olive oil. Add ¼ cup (½ oz/155 g) torn frisée, season with salt and pepper, and squeeze over the juice of 1 lemon half. Toss gently and transfer to a platter. Scatter a small amount of shaved Parmesan cheese on top and serve right away. Serves 4.

Artichokes with Herbed Yogurt Sauce

Arrange 4 trimmed large artichokes, stem end up, in a single layer in a steamer basket and steam over simmering water until the bottoms can be easily pierced with a knife, 30–40 minutes. In a bowl, mix together 1 cup (8 oz/250 g) nonfat plain yogurt, 1 cup (1 oz/30 g) chopped fresh herbs, 1 chopped green onion, 1 small drop agave nectar, and salt and hot pepper sauce to taste. Serve the artichokes with the dipping sauce. Serves 4.

Braised Artichokes with Lemon & Garlic

Trim the fuzzy tips from 6 large artichokes. Halve them lengthwise and, using a melon baller or small spoon, remove the fuzzy choke. Place the artichokes in a saucepan with the juice of ½ lemon. Add 10 halved garlic cloves, 5 fresh thyme sprigs, 2 bay leaves, ½ teaspoon salt, and ¼ cup (2 fl oz/60 ml) olive oil. Add water to cover and bring to a boil over medium-high heat, reduce the heat to medium, and simmer for 5 minutes. Remove from the heat and let cool in the pan, about 1 hour or until tender when pierced with a knife. Sprinkle with chopped fresh parsley and serve right away. Serves 6.

Artichokes Vinaigrette

Trim 1¼ lb (625 g) baby artichokes, arrange in a single layer in a steamer basket, and steam over simmering water until the bottoms can be easily pierced with a knife, 8–10 minutes. Let cool, then arrange in a single layer in a baking dish. Drizzle with 3 tablespoons olive oil and roast in a 400°F (200°C) oven until lightly browned, 10–12 minutes. Pour in 1 tablespoon red wine vinegar, 2 teaspoons minced fresh oregano, ½ clove minced garlic, and salt and pepper to taste. Let stand for a few minutes to blend the flavors. Serves 4.

Toasted spices infuse this crunchy salad of grated root vegetables with their warmth. Harissa, a North African chile-and-spice paste, adds a suggestion of heat to this unique version of crudités.

Moroccan-Style Carrot & Parsnip Salad

MAKES 6 SERVINGS

$1/4$ teaspoon ground cinnamon

$1/4$ teaspoon ground cumin

$1/4$ teaspoon ground coriander

$1/8$ teaspoon ground ginger

3 large carrots (about $3/4$ lb/375 g total weight)

3 large parsnips (about $3/4$ lb/375 g total weight)

$1/4$ cup (2 fl oz/60 ml) fresh lemon juice

1 tablespoon honey

$3/4$ teaspoon prepared harissa

Sea salt and freshly ground pepper

6 tablespoons (3 fl oz/90 ml) extra-virgin olive oil

$1/2$ cup (2 oz/60 g) roasted shelled pistachio nuts, coarsely chopped

$2/3$ cup (4 oz/125 g) raisins

$1/4$ cup ($1/3$ oz/10 g) coarsely chopped fresh cilantro or mint

In a small, heavy frying pan over medium-low heat, combine the cinnamon, cumin, coriander, and ginger and toast, stirring constantly, until fragrant, about 2 minutes. Remove from the heat and let cool to room temperature.

Peel the carrots and parsnips and shred them on the large holes of a box grater-shredder. Set aside.

In a small nonreactive bowl, whisk together the toasted spices, lemon juice, honey, harissa, and a scant $1/2$ teaspoon salt. Slowly whisk in the olive oil to make a dressing. Taste and adjust the seasoning.

In a bowl, stir together the pistachios and a pinch of salt. Add the carrots and parsnips, raisins, $1/2$ teaspoon salt, several grindings of pepper, and the dressing and toss well. Taste and adjust the seasoning. Transfer to a platter or serving bowl, sprinkle with the cilantro, and serve right away.

Anchovies are loaded with omega-3 fatty acids. They are also wonderful to keep on hand for adding unique, savory flavor to a variety of dishes, including this side of lightly sautéed dark greens, onions, and tomatoes.

Swiss Chard with Tomato, Lemon & Anchovy

MAKES 4 SERVINGS

1 large bunch Swiss chard

3 tablespoons olive oil

$^3/_4$ cup (6 fl oz/180 ml) low-sodium vegetable or chicken broth

2 or 3 anchovy fillets, rinsed and patted dry

2 tablespoons fresh lemon juice

Freshly ground pepper

$^1/_2$ yellow onion, chopped

2 ripe plum tomatoes, seeded and chopped

Separate the stems from the chard leaves by cutting along both sides of the center vein. Stack the leaves, roll them up lengthwise, and cut crosswise into strips about $^3/_4$ inch (2 cm) wide. Trim off the tough bottoms from the stems and cut crosswise into $^1/_2$-inch (12-mm) pieces.

In a frying pan, heat 1 tablespoon of the olive oil over medium-high heat. Add the chard stems and sauté for 5 minutes. Add $^1/_4$ cup (2 fl oz/60 ml) of the broth and cook until the stems are tender and the pan is almost dry, 3–4 minutes. Remove from the heat. Push the chard stems to one side of the pan and add the anchovies to the other. Using the back of a wooden spoon, mash the anchovies until creamy, then stir in the chard stems along with the lemon juice. Season with pepper. Arrange the cooked chard stems on one side of a warmed platter.

In a clean frying pan over medium-high heat, heat the remaining 2 tablespoons olive oil. Add the onion and sauté until golden, 6–7 minutes. Add the chard leaves a few handfuls at a time, stirring each batch until wilted. Add the tomatoes and the remaining $^1/_2$ cup (4 fl oz/125 ml) broth and cook, stirring occasionally, until the chard is tender, about 10 minutes. Spoon the leaves onto the platter with the stems. Serve right away.

Earthy quinoa, pleasantly bitter radicchio, sweet-tart dried cherries, and crunchy pistachios combine in this unexpectedly delicious salad. Be generous with the basil if you like an herbal edge to the dish.

Quinoa & Radicchio Salad with Dried Cherries & Nuts

MAKES 4 SERVINGS

1 cup (8 oz/250 g) quinoa

$^1/_2$ head radicchio (about 4 oz/125 g), cored and thinly sliced

$^1/_4$ cup (2 fl oz/60 ml) balsamic vinegar

2 tablespoons olive oil

$^1/_4$ cup (1 oz/30 g) dried tart cherries

$^1/_4$ cup (1 oz/30 g) shelled roasted pistachios, chopped

3 tablespoons chopped fresh flat-leaf parsley

Sea salt and freshly ground pepper

Torn fresh basil for garnish

Put the quinoa in a fine-mesh strainer. Rinse thoroughly under running cold water and drain. In a saucepan, bring 2 cups (16 fl oz/500 ml) water to a boil over high heat. Add the quinoa, stir once, and reduce the heat to low. Cover and cook, without stirring, until all the water has been absorbed and the grains are tender, about 15 minutes. Let stand for 5 minutes, covered, then fluff with a fork and transfer to a large bowl.

Add the radicchio, vinegar, olive oil, cherries, pistachios, and parsley to the warm quinoa and stir gently to mix and coat well. Season with salt and pepper. Sprinkle with basil and serve warm or at room temperature.

desserts

This cobbler shows how to reduce the amount of butter used in the topping by replacing part of it with buttermilk and other lean ingredients. Halving instead of slicing the strawberries keeps them from turning mushy in the filling.

Three-Berry Cobbler

MAKES 6 SERVINGS

Canola-oil spray

2 cups (8 oz/250 g) blueberries

4 cups (1 lb/500 g) raspberries

4 cups (1 lb/500 g) strawberries, hulled and halved lengthwise

$1/4$ cup ($2^1/2$ oz/75 g) raspberry jam

1 tablespoon instant tapioca

$1/2$ cup ($2^1/2$ oz/75 g) whole-wheat flour

$1/2$ cup ($2^1/2$ oz/75 g) unbleached all-purpose flour

2 teaspoons baking powder

$1/4$ teaspoon baking soda

$1/2$ teaspoon sea salt

3 tablespoons unsalted butter, at room temperature

$1/3$ cup (3 oz/90 g) sugar

$1/3$ cup (3 fl oz/80 ml) nonfat buttermilk

Preheat the oven to 350°F (180°C). Coat an 8-inch (20-cm) square nonreactive metal pan or ceramic baking dish lightly with the canola-oil spray. (Do not use a glass dish for this recipe.)

To make the filling, in a bowl, combine the blueberries, raspberries, strawberries, jam, and tapioca. Using a rubber spatula, stir gently to coat the berries with the jam. Spread the fruit in an even layer in the prepared pan.

To make the topping, in a bowl, whisk together the flours, baking powder, baking soda, and salt. In a bowl, using a handheld mixer, beat together the butter and sugar on high speed until fluffy and pale, about 3 minutes. Reduce the speed to medium and beat in about half of the buttermilk. Add about half of the dry ingredients and beat until almost combined. Beat in the remaining buttermilk. Add the remaining dry ingredients and beat until a thick, sticky batter forms. Do not overmix.

Drop the batter by heaping spoonfuls over the fruit. Spread it as evenly as possible, using the back of the spoon. Some of the fruit will be exposed.

Bake the cobbler until the crust is deep golden brown and the fruit juices bubble up around the edges and through any cracks, about 40 minutes. Transfer to a wire rack and let cool to lukewarm before serving. Scoop the cobbler from the dish onto dessert plates and serve.

Fresh basil is unusual to find in desserts, but in this icy granita, it pairs perfectly with ripe cantaloupe. Be sure to use quality, ripe produce to make the best-tasting granita, especially since the recipe calls for so few ingredients.

Cantaloupe-Basil Granita

MAKES 8 SERVINGS

30 fresh basil leaves

$^1/_4$ cup (2 fl oz/60 ml) fresh lime juice

$^2/_3$ cup (5 oz/155 g) sugar

1 ripe cantaloupe (about 4 lb/2 kg)

Coarsely chop 20 basil leaves; set the remaining 10 leaves aside. In a small nonreactive saucepan, combine the lime juice, sugar, and 2 tablespoons water and bring to a simmer over medium-high heat. Simmer, swirling occasionally, until the sugar is dissolved, about 2 minutes. Remove from the heat, stir in the chopped basil, cover, and let steep for 15 minutes.

Meanwhile, halve the cantaloupe and scoop out and discard the seeds. Cut off the rind and then cut the flesh into 1-inch (2.5-cm) cubes.

Strain the basil mixture through a fine-mesh sieve into a blender. Add half of the melon cubes and pulse a few times, then purée until smooth. Add the remaining melon cubes and pulse a few times, then add the reserved whole basil leaves and purée until the mixture is smooth. Pour the mixture into a 13-by-9-by-2-inch (33-by-23-by-5-cm) glass baking dish. Cover with plastic wrap, place on a rimmed baking sheet, and place in the freezer.

After 1–1½ hours, check the granita. When the mixture starts to freeze around the edges of the dish, stir it with a fork, then return the dish to the freezer. Stir the granita with the fork every 45 minutes or so, until the mixture is completely frozen into icy grains and the texture is fluffy, 2–3 hours longer.

Spoon the granita into bowls and serve right away. (The granita is best when eaten within 2 days. If it becomes very hard and dry in the freezer, let it stand at room temperature for 10–15 minutes before serving.)

Eat for Maximum Hydration

Nearly 90 percent water, melons are also rich in nutrients, including fiber, and low in calories, making them a high-value food that can help you maintain your weight. Watermelons are high in vitamin C and contain the antioxidant lycopene. Cantaloupes boast high amounts of vitamins C and A as well as potassium. Honeydew contains similar nutrients to cantaloupe, but less of them.

Serve melons all day, as they are appropriate for any meal from breakfast to desserts after dinner. Their nutrition-dense and calorie-light qualities also make them terrific for snacks, whether on their own or embellished with spices.

Four Ways to Use Melons

Cantaloupe Agua Fresca
In a blender, combine 4 cups (1½ lb/750 g) seeded and cubed cantaloupe, ⅓ cup (3 fl oz/80 ml) fresh lime juice, ¼ cup (¼ oz/7 g) lightly packed fresh mint leaves, and agave nectar to taste. Blend on high speed until the melon is completely liquefied and the mixture is smooth. Transfer to a pitcher and stir in 4 cups (64 fl oz/1 l) water. Pour over ice to serve. Serves 4–6.

Grilled Prosciutto-Wrapped Honeydew
Wrap wedges of honeydew melon in prosciutto, trimming off the fat from the ham, if you like. Brush lightly with olive oil and grill over medium heat until the fruit is warm and the prosciutto is lightly browned. Serve as a starter or as an accompaniment to an arugula salad. Servings vary.

Watermelon with Chile Salt
In a small bowl, gently stir together 1 teaspoon red pepper flakes, 1 teaspoon grated lime zest, and 1 tablespoon coarse salt. Sprinkle the chile salt on 6 watermelon wedges. Serve right away. Serves 6.

Watermelon-Lime Ice Pops
In a blender or food processor, combine 4 cups (24 oz/750 g) cubed seedless watermelon, 2 teaspoons agave nectar, 2 tablespoons fresh lime juice, and a pinch of salt and blend until very smooth. Divide the purée among ice pop molds and freeze until partially frozen, about 1 hour. If using sticks, insert them and continue to freeze until solid, at least 3 hours or up to 3 days. Makes 6–10, depending on the size of the molds.

In this unusual Spanish version of chocolate mousse,
extra-virgin olive oil replaces the usual cream, resulting
in a silky texture and a hint of the oil's flavor. Use a mild-
tasting oil to let the flavor of the chocolate shine through.

Olive Oil Chocolate Mousse

MAKES 4 SERVINGS

6 oz (185 g) bittersweet chocolate,
finely chopped

3 large egg yolks

$1/4$ cup (2 fl oz/60 ml) mild-flavored extra-
virgin olive oil

3 tablespoons warm water

$1/4$ teaspoon sea salt

2 large egg whites

$1/8$ teaspoon cream of tartar

$1/4$ cup (2 oz/60 g) sugar

Chocolate shavings
for serving (optional)

In a heatproof bowl set over, but not touching, a pan of barely simmering water,
stir the chocolate until melted and smooth. Remove from the heat and whisk
in the egg yolks, olive oil, warm water, and salt until well blended.

In a clean bowl, using an electric mixer set on medium-high speed, beat the
egg whites with the cream of tartar until frothy. Add the sugar and continue
beating until the mixture forms soft peaks. Fold about one-third of the egg-white
mixture into the chocolate mixture until no white streaks remain. Gently fold
in the remaining egg-white mixture until well incorporated.

Spoon the mousse into 4 custard cups, dividing it evenly, and refrigerate until
well chilled, at least 4 hours or up to overnight.

Sprinkle with the chocolate shavings. Serve right away.

*Note: This recipe contains raw eggs. If you have health and safety concerns, you may
wish to avoid foods made with raw eggs.*

Although most kinds of berries can be found year-round, most of them often taste best in the spring and summer. Plump berries with deep color have the most flavor. You can also spoon this over slices of angel food cake.

Warm Berry Compote

MAKES 4 SERVINGS

$1/2$ cup (4 oz/125 g) sugar

2 cups (8 oz/250 g) strawberries, hulled and quartered

1 cup (4 oz/125 g) blueberries

1 cup (4 oz/125 g) blackberries

2 teaspoons fresh lemon juice

Pinch of sea salt

2 tablespoons unsalted butter, at room temperature, cut into cubes

Good-quality vanilla frozen yogurt for serving

In a large, nonreactive sauté pan over medium heat, combine the sugar and $1/4$ cup (2 fl oz/60 ml) water and bring to a boil, stirring to dissolve the sugar. Cook for 2 minutes, then add the strawberries, blueberries, blackberries, lemon juice, and salt. Return to a boil, add the butter, and swirl the mixture in the pan until the butter melts.

Put scoops of frozen yogurt in dessert bowls and spoon the compote over the top, scooping up both berries and sauce. Serve right away.

This is a perfect way to showcase any kind of summer-ripe melon. The ingredients may surprise you, but the cayenne pepper provides a touch of contrasting heat and a pinch of sea salt brings out the sweetness in the fruit.

Sweet & Spicy Melon with Lime

MAKES 4–6 SERVINGS

$1/2$ cup (6 fl oz/180 ml) honey

$1/4$ cup (2 fl oz/60 ml) fresh lime juice

$1/8$ teaspoon cayenne pepper

1 teaspoon grated lime zest

$1/2$ small seedless watermelon (about 3 lb/1.5 kg)

1 ripe small cantaloupe (about 3 lb/1.5 kg)

Pinch of sea salt

2–3 tablespoons torn fresh mint

In a small saucepan over medium-high heat, combine the honey, lime juice, and cayenne pepper. Bring to a boil, then reduce the heat to low and simmer for 3 minutes to blend the flavors. Remove from the heat and let cool to lukewarm. Stir in the lime zest. Let cool to room temperature.

Cut the rind from the watermelon and then cut the flesh into bite-sized cubes. Halve the cantaloupe. Scoop out the seeds and discard. Cut off the rind and then cut the flesh into cubes.

Place all of the melon in a wide, shallow serving bowl and drizzle with half of the honey-lime syrup. Toss gently to coat, then drizzle with the remaining syrup. Sprinkle with the salt and mint and serve right away.

This recipe works with any type of stone fruits, but plums go particularly well with the exotic flavors of star anise. You could also make these for a brunch, served over pancakes or with hot cereal, or layered in a parfait with nonfat yogurt and granola.

Roasted Spiced Black Plums

MAKES 4–6 SERVINGS

Canola-oil spray
8 ripe black plums, halved and pitted
1 tablespoon brown sugar
8 star anise pods
Nonfat or low-fat vanilla frozen yogurt
for serving

Preheat the oven to 400°F (200°C). Coat a baking dish just large enough to hold the plum halves in a single layer lightly with the canola-oil spray.

Arrange the plums, cut side up, in the prepared dish. Cut a thin slice off the round side of each half to help them sit flat, if you like. Sprinkle brown sugar over each plum half, dividing evenly, then sprinkle the star anise pods evenly over the top. Roast until the sugar has melted, the plums are warmed through, and the skins are just beginning to wrinkle a bit on the edges, about 15 minutes. Let cool to warm, or use right away.

To serve, put scoops of frozen yogurt in 4 dessert bowls, arrange 2 plum halves on top of each (discard the star anise), and serve right away.

Baked summer fruit is irresistible when topped with a crumbly almond streusel topping. Substitute peaches or plums if you wish. For a delightful contrast in temperature, serve the warm nectarines with dollops of cold nonfat vanilla yogurt.

Baked Nectarines with Cinnamon-Almond Streusel

MAKES 4 SERVINGS

Canola-oil spray

4 ripe but firm nectarines, halved and pitted

6 tablespoons (2 oz/60 g) whole-wheat flour

6 tablespoons ($2^{1}/_{2}$ oz/75 g) firmly packed brown sugar

$^{1}/_{2}$ teaspoon ground cinnamon

$^{1}/_{8}$ teaspoon sea salt

2 tablespoons unsalted butter, cut into pieces

$^{1}/_{3}$ cup (2 oz/60 g) roasted almonds, chopped

Preheat the oven to 400°F (200°C). Coat a 9-by-13-inch (23-by-33-cm) baking dish lightly with the canola-oil spray.

Arrange the nectarines, cut side up, in the prepared dish. Cut a thin slice off the round side of each half to help them sit flat, if you like. Set aside.

In a food processor, combine the flour, brown sugar, cinnamon, and salt and pulse a few times to mix. Add the butter pieces and pulse just until the mixture resembles coarse crumbs. Do not overmix. Stir in the almonds. Squeeze the flour-sugar-butter mixture into small handfuls and distribute it evenly over the nectarine halves, pressing it lightly to adhere.

Bake until the nectarines are tender when pierced with a small knife and the topping is nicely browned, about 20 minutes. Arrange 2 nectarine halves on each of 4 dessert plates and serve warm.

In this recipe, fresh bay leaves lend their intriguing aroma, usually reserved for savory dishes, to a simple dessert of honeyed pears flavored with almond-scented amaretto, toasted nuts, and tart Greek-style yogurt.

Bay-Scented Roasted Pears with Honey & Greek Yogurt

MAKES 6 SERVINGS

$1/3$ cup ($1^1/_2$ oz/45 g) slivered almonds

3 ripe but firm Bosc pears

$1/3$ cup ($4^1/_2$ fl oz/140 ml) honey

4 fresh bay leaves

3 tablespoons unsalted butter, cut into 6 pieces

2 tablespoons amaretto liqueur

$1^1/_2$ cups (12 oz/375 g) nonfat or low-fat plain Greek-style yogurt

Preheat the oven to 375°F (190°C). Place the almonds on a rimmed baking sheet and toast in the oven, stirring once or twice, until fragrant and lightly browned, 5–6 minutes. Immediately pour onto a plate to cool. Leave the oven on.

Halve the pears lengthwise. Using a melon baller, scoop out the cores.

In a small Dutch oven or heavy ovenproof saucepan, combine the honey and bay leaves and bring to a simmer over medium-high heat. Reduce the heat to medium and continue to simmer, stirring occasionally, until the honey is fragrant and turns a rich amber color, about 3 minutes. Remove from the heat.

Place the butter pieces in the pot with the honey, spacing them evenly. Using tongs, carefully place a pear half, cut side down, on top of each piece of butter. Cover the pot and roast the pears in the oven for 10 minutes. Using the tongs, gently turn the pears over. Switch to a long-handled spoon and baste the pears with the honey mixture. Drizzle the pears with the amaretto and continue to roast, uncovered, until golden brown and a sharp knife slips easily into the centers, 6–8 minutes longer. Remove from the oven and let the pears cool slightly in the honey mixture, about 30 minutes.

In a bowl, whisk the yogurt until smooth. To serve, arrange the pear halves on a platter, drizzle the honey mixture from the pot over the top, and sprinkle with the toasted almonds. Serve right away, passing the yogurt at the table.

Fresh-Picked Nutrients

Pears contain 5 grams of fiber as well as potassium, vitamin C, folic acid, and antioxidants. Their high water content promotes fullness, so pears such as Bartlett and Bosc are great to have on hand as snacks during their prime season in fall and winter. Pears need to be picked green, then ripened off the tree. For fullest flavor, set them on the counter until they yield when gently pressed near the stem.

Adaptable pears go well with a range of different ingredients. Try them raw as a sweet contrast to tart cranberries in a fresh relish, or sliced as part of a salad. Roasted, pears complement sweet vegetables and help offset savory meats and poultry with their bright flavor.

Four Ways to Use Pears

Pear, Orange & Cranberry Relish

In a food processor, process 1 thin-skinned navel orange, halved and cut into thin wedges (including peel); 3 cups cranberries; and 2–3 tablespoons sugar until finely chopped. Transfer to a bowl and stir in 2 firm but ripe pears, peeled, cored, and finely chopped, and ½ teaspoon ground cardamom. Mix well and refrigerate for about 1 hour before serving. Serve with roasted poultry or meat. Makes about 4 cups (32 fl oz/1 l).

Pear & Fennel Salad

In a large bowl, whisk together 1 tablespoon sherry vinegar, 2 tablespoons extra-virgin olive oil, 1 tablespoon coarsely grated pecorino Romano cheese, and salt and pepper to taste. Add 1 bulb fennel, shaved, and toss to coat. Arrange on each plate 1½ cups (1½ oz/45 g) baby arugula leaves and top with some fennel mixture. Top each salad with ½ pear, halved, cored, and thinly sliced. Sprinkle each with 1 tablespoon dried currants. Serves 4.

Pears & Parsnips with Almonds

On a rimmed baking sheet, arrange 1 lb (500 g) parsnips, peeled and quartered, and 3 Bosc or Anjou pears, quartered lengthwise and cored. Sprinkle with 3 tablespoons olive oil and salt to taste, then toss to coat evenly. Spread out in an even layer and roast in a 400°F (200°C) oven until tender when pierced with a small knife and browned, 30–40 minutes. Top with 3 tablespoons toasted almonds and serve right away. Serves 6.

Savory Roasted Pears

Oil a shallow baking dish and drizzle 1 tablespoon maple syrup into the dish. Arrange 4 firm but ripe Bosc, Bartlett, or Anjou pears, halved lengthwise and cored, in the dish, cut-side up. Brush the cut sides with fresh lemon juice and sprinkle with 1 tablespoon chopped fresh sage. Drizzle the pears with 2 tablespoons dry white wine. Roast in a 425°F (220°C) oven until just tender, 22–25 minutes. Drizzle with 2 tablespoons additional wine and ¼ cup (2 fl oz/ 60 ml) water. Continue to roast, basting 1 or 2 times, until the pears are very tender and lightly browned, 12–15 minutes. Serve warm or at room temperature drizzled with the pan juices. Serves 4 as a side dish.

Baked apples stuffed with dried fruits are an alluring dessert. Honey makes a sparkling glaze for the apples. When choosing apricots, avoid the Turkish variety, as they are too sweet. Unsulfered California dried apricots are a good choice.

Baked Apples Filled with Dried Fruits

MAKES 4 SERVINGS

16 dried apricots

4 dried Calimyrna figs

4 soft pitted prunes

2 dried pear halves, each cut into 4 pieces

$1/4$ cup (1 oz/30 g) dried cranberries

$1/4$ cup ($1^1/2$ oz/45 g) raisins

$1^1/3$ cups (11 fl oz/330 ml) unfiltered apple cider

4 baking apples such as Rome Beauty, Fuji, or Jonagold

$1/3$ cup ($4^1/2$ fl oz/140 ml) honey

In a heatproof bowl, combine the apricots, figs, prunes, pears, cranberries, and raisins. In a small saucepan, bring 1 cup (8 fl oz/250 ml) of the cider to a boil. Pour the hot liquid over the fruits. Let stand until the fruits have plumped, 30–60 minutes.

Preheat the oven to 350°F (180°C).

Cut a slice ½ inch (12 mm) thick off the stem end of each apple. Using a melon baller, scoop out and discard the core from each apple, being careful not to puncture the base of the fruit. Then, carve out the flesh to leave a shell about ½ inch (12 mm) thick. Discard the flesh or reserve for another use. Stand the apples in a baking dish just large enough to hold them upright.

Drain the plumped fruits in a sieve held over the baking dish. Spoon the fruits into the apple cavities, dividing them evenly. Drape squares of aluminum foil over the stuffing in each apple and bake until a knife pierces the bottom of the apples with only slight resistance, 35–40 minutes. Remove from the oven and lift off the foil.

When the apples are cool enough to handle, after about 20 minutes, use a slotted spoon to transfer them to a platter. Spoon any of the fruit stuffing that fell off back in place. Discard the liquid remaining in the dish.

In a saucepan, combine the remaining ⅓ cup (3 fl oz/80 ml) apple cider and the honey. Bring to a boil over medium-high heat, reduce the heat to medium, and simmer until the liquid is syrupy and reduced by about one-third, about 8 minutes. Spoon the hot glaze over the stuffing and apples until it pools in the bottom of the platter. Serve warm or at room temperature.

Naturally sweet and creamy when frozen, bananas are full of potassium. Cover them with dark chocolate and nuts and you have a quick, healthy treat. Choose bright yellow bananas that are not too ripe and freckled but rather still have some firmness.

Dark Chocolate–Banana Pops with Roasted Almonds

MAKES ABOUT 30 POPS; SERVES 8

12 oz (375 g) bittersweet chocolate, chopped

$^2/_3$ cup (4 oz/125 g) roasted almonds or pecans, chopped

2 ripe bananas

In a bowl set over a pan of barely simmering water, melt the chocolate, stirring occasionally, until smooth. Remove the pan from the heat, but leave the bowl of chocolate on top to keep warm.

Put the nuts in a small bowl. Line a baking sheet with waxed paper.

Peel the bananas and cut them into ½-inch (12-mm) rounds. Drop 1 banana slice at a time into the chocolate and turn to coat. Lift out with a fork, tapping the fork gently on the bowl edge to allow excess chocolate to drip back into the bowl. Place the banana slice on the prepared baking sheet and sprinkle with nuts. Repeat to dip and coat the remaining banana slices.

Freeze the coated bananas until the chocolate is set, about 20 minutes, then transfer to an airtight container and store in the freezer for up to 1 week.

A syrup flavored with cardamom offers hints of ginger, allspice, clove, and black pepper, to complement the tropical sweetness of creamy-textured mangoes. Used sparingly, whipped cream adds a touch of indulgence to an otherwise fat-free dessert.

Spiced Mango Pavlovas

MAKES 6 SERVINGS

4 large egg whites, at room temperature

$^{1}/_{8}$ teaspoon cream of tartar

$1^{1}/_{2}$ cups (12 oz/375 g) sugar

1 tablespoon cornstarch

5 whole green cardamom pods

3 ripe mangoes, peeled and cut into $^{1}/_{2}$-inch (12-mm) cubes (see page 48)

Finely grated zest and juice of 1 lime

Sweetened Whipped Cream for serving (page 219)

Preheat the oven to 275°F (135°C). Line a baking sheet with parchment paper.

In a stand mixer, beat the egg whites on high speed until foamy. Add the cream of tartar and continue to beat while gradually adding 1 cup (8 oz/250 g) of the sugar until soft peaks form. Sift the cornstarch over the whites and fold in gently. Spoon 6 dollops of the mixture onto the prepared sheet, dividing it evenly and spacing the mounds about 3 inches (7.5 cm) apart. Using the back of a spoon and working in a circular motion, spread each dollop into a disk about 4 inches (10 cm) in diameter. Finally, make a depression in the center of each. Bake the meringues until they are no longer tacky on the surface and are very lightly golden, about 1 hour. Set the baking sheet on a wire rack and let the meringues cool completely on the pan.

Using the flat side of a chef's knife, lightly crack open the cardamom pods. Add the pods to a saucepan along with the remaining $^{1}/_{2}$ cup (4 oz/125 g) sugar and 2 tablespoons water and bring to a simmer over medium-high heat. Simmer, swirling occasionally, until the sugar is dissolved, about 2 minutes. Let cool to room temperature.

Put the mangoes in a bowl. Squeeze the lime juice over the mangoes, pour the cardamom syrup through a fine-mesh sieve into the bowl, and stir to mix well.

To serve, place each of the meringues on a dessert plate. Spoon a small amount of whipped cream on top of each meringue. Using a slotted spoon, top the whipped cream with some of the mango cubes. Drizzle a little cardamom syrup over the top, sprinkle with lime zest, and serve right away.

Pearl tapioca is a gluten-free starch. While it is not nutritionally dense, it does provide some minerals and fiber. Here it is made into an immunity-boosting pudding with coconut milk and fresh mango and papaya.

Tapioca Pudding with Tropical Fruits

MAKES 4–6 SERVINGS

$1/2$ cup (3 oz/90 g) small pearl tapioca

$1/4$ cup (2 fl oz/60 ml) unsweetened coconut milk

2 tablespoons granulated sugar

1 ripe mango, peeled and diced

$1/2$ ripe medium or large papaya, peeled, seeded, and sliced

Juice of 1 lime

4 teaspoons raw sugar

In a saucepan, bring 4 cups (32 fl oz/1 l) water to a boil over high heat. Reduce the heat to medium, add the tapioca, and simmer gently until translucent, 12–15 minutes. Drain thoroughly through a fine-mesh sieve.

Put the tapioca in a bowl. Add the coconut milk and granulated sugar and stir to mix well and help dissolve the sugar. Cover and refrigerate until well chilled, at least 1 hour and up to 24 hours.

To serve, divide the pudding among dessert bowls and top with the fruit. Drizzle with the lime juice, sprinkle with the raw sugar, and serve right away.

Think Blue for Health

Eating blueberries benefits your heart and helps to stabilize blood pressure. It may boost your memory, as well. Blueberries' power and intense color come from antioxidants called anthocyanins, along with fiber, vitamin C and manganese. Dark, evenly colored blueberries are best. A silver sheen on the berry indicates just-picked freshness—it disappears after a few days.

Blueberries are popular at the breakfast table, often seen in pancakes, muffins, or other baked goods. Their bold color also helps create eye-catching drinks, salads, and vibrant main-course sauces. Layered with nonfat yogurt, honey, and nuts, they also make an easy and healthful dessert.

Four Ways to Use Blueberries

Sparkling Blueberry Lemonade

In a blender, combine the juice of 1 lemon, 1 tablespoon honey, and ¼ cup (1 oz/30 g) blueberries and blend to a smooth purée. Fill a glass with ice, pour in the blueberry purée, and top with a splash of sparkling water. Serves 1.

Blueberry, Almond & Feta Salad

In a large bowl, whisk together 3 tablespoons extra-virgin olive oil, 4 teaspoons raspberry vinegar, and salt and pepper to taste. Add 1 minced shallot, 1½ cups (6 oz/185 g) blueberries, and 2 teaspoons chopped fresh chives. Let stand for 10–15 minutes, then add 1 head butter lettuce, torn, and 3 oz (90 g) crumbled feta cheese and toss well. Serve right away topped with ¼ cup (1½ oz/45 g) toasted almonds. Serves 4.

Wasabi-Spiked Blueberry-Rhubarb Sauce

Heat 1 tablespoon canola oil in a sauté pan over medium-high heat. Add ½ minced red onion and sauté until tender. Add 2–3 thin rhubarb stalks, sliced, and cook, stirring, until the bottom of the pan looks syrupy, 3–4 minutes. Add 1½ cups (6 oz/185 g) blueberries and 2 tablespoons honey. When the berries start to soften, after about 1 minute, reduce the heat to medium. Simmer until the rhubarb is tender and collapsing, about 5 minutes. Remove from the heat and stir in ¼ teaspoon wasabi powder. Serve warm with grilled or roasted salmon, pork, or poultry. Serves 4.

Blueberry-Yogurt Parfaits

For each parfait, spoon ½ cup (4 oz/125 g) plain low-fat or nonfat Greek-style yogurt into a glass. Spoon about ½ cup (2 oz/60 g) blueberries over the yogurt. Sprinkle with 1–2 teaspoons toasted sliced almonds and ½ teaspoon honey. Repeat the layers, ending with the honey. Serves 1 or more.

The lemony-herbal nuances of lemongrass are infused into a sweet syrup and then paired with juicy raspberries in this exotic twist on a classic dessert. It's delicious on its own, but if you feel like splurging, serve with lightly sweetened whipped cream.

Raspberries in Lemongrass Syrup

MAKES 6 SERVINGS

1 stalk fresh lemongrass
$^1/_3$ cup (3 oz/90 g) sugar
8 cups (2 lb/1 kg) raspberries
Nonfat plain Greek-style yogurt
for serving

Remove the dry outer leaves of the lemongrass and then trim the stalk to a 3-inch (7.5-cm) piece of the pale green bottom section. Using the back of the blade of a chef's knife, bruise the lemongrass, flattening the stalk and breaking some of the fibers to release its aroma.

In a small saucepan, combine the sugar and $^1/_3$ cup (3 fl oz/80 ml) water and bring to a simmer over medium-high heat. Simmer, swirling occasionally, until the sugar is dissolved, about 2 minutes. Remove from the heat, add the lemongrass, cover, and let steep until cooled completely, about 30 minutes.

Strain the lemongrass syrup through a fine-mesh sieve into a large bowl, pressing on the stalk with the back of a spoon to extract as much syrup as possible; discard the lemongrass.

Add the raspberries to the syrup and stir gently. Divide the raspberries and syrup among 6 dessert bowls. Top with the yogurt and serve right away.

glossary

antibacterial

Helping to destroy or inhibit the growth of bacteria. Ingredients with antibacterial properties include garlic and some fresh herbs, such as peppermint.

anti-inflammatory

Helping to reduce or prevent inflammation in the body tissues. Anti-inflammatory ingredients include deeply pigmented fruits and vegetables, spices such as turmeric, and fresh herbs.

antimicrobial

Helping to destroy or inhibit the growth of microbes, such as salmonella. Ingredients with antimicrobial properties include some alliums and fresh herbs like basil and cilantro.

antioxidants

Antioxidants protect against and repair daily damage to our cells and tissues. They have also been linked to heart health and cancer prevention. Some come in the form of vitamins, such as vitamins C and E. Others are compounds found in plant foods such as phytonutrients like lycopene and beta-carotene, or polyphenols such as ellagic acid. The best sources of antioxidants are colorful fruits, vegetables, nuts, and whole grains.

carbohydrates

There are three main kinds of carbohydrates: starch, sugar, and fiber. Starch and sugar provide our bodies and brains with energy. Although our bodies can't digest fiber, it provides a number of significant benefits. The healthiest sources of carbohydrates are fruits, vegetables, beans, and whole grains such as whole-wheat bread and pasta, brown rice, and quinoa.

capsaicin

The substance in chiles that makes them hot. Capsaicin has a host of health benefits, and is thought to help speed metabolism, relieve pain, fight cancer, and more.

carotenoids

Carotenoids are colored pigments in plants that provide multiple health benefits such as improved vision, enhanced immunity, or protection against cancer. While beta-carotene, the pigment that gives carrots their orange color, is perhaps the most well known carotenoid, others include lycopene from tomatoes and zeaxanthin and lutein from spinach.

cholesterol

Foods from animal sources such as eggs, milk, cheese, and meat contain cholesterol, but the human body makes its own supply as well. While cholesterol in our diets was once thought to be a major contributor to high cholesterol levels, we now know that foods rich in saturated fat raise unhealthy LDL cholesterol in our blood streams more substantially than cholesterol from other food. Plant compounds like phytosterols in wheat germ, peanuts, and almonds and beta-glucan from oats have been shown to lower cholesterol.

fats

Our bodies need fat to absorb certain vitamins, build the membranes that line our cells, and cushion our joints and organs. But fats aren't all created equal. Saturated and hydrogenated fat are linked to chronic ailments such as heart disease, while unsaturated fats can be more healthful.

monounsaturated fats Found in nuts, avocados, olive oil, and canola oil, these fats are less likely to raise levels of unhealthy LDL cholesterol, linked to heart attack and stroke. They also help keep arteries clear by maintaining levels of healthy HDL cholesterol.

polyunsaturated fats These fats can play an important role in helping control cholesterol. While most of us get plenty of the polyunsaturated fat linolenic acid from vegetable, corn, and soybean oil, our diets don't usually contain enough of heart-healthy omega-3 fats. These are found as EPA and DHA in fish or in the form of alpha linolenic acid in flaxseed, canola oil, and walnuts.

saturated fats Found in meats, dairy products, and tropical oils such as coconut oil and palm oil, these fats raise blood levels of unhealthy LDL cholesterol.

trans fats Present in hydrogenated vegetable oils in many processed and fried foods, trans fats may be even more harmful than saturated fats.

fiber

Fiber is the component of plant foods that our bodies can't digest. Insoluble fiber does not dissolve in water and is known for preventing constipation. Soluble fiber softens in water and helps lower blood cholesterol levels. Fiber-rich diets have been linked with improved digestive health and reduced risk for type 2 diabetes and heart disease.

flavonoids

These plant compounds help prevent heart disease and possibly cancer. They include quercetin from onions and apples, anthocyanidins from berries, and isoflavones from soy.

free radicals

These unstable molecules act to damage healthy cells and to cause inflammation in body tissues. Eating antioxidants can help counteract their damage.

glycemic index

A method of measuring the effects of various foods on blood sugar. Foods that quickly raise blood sugar levels rate high on the index, while foods that slowly act on blood sugar rate near the bottom. Foods that produce a slow but sustained release of sugar in the bloodstream are considered best for optimum health.

lycopene

A carotenoid believed to protect against heart disease and some types of cancer. It is found in tomatoes and other red fruits and vegetables.

minerals

Minerals are elements that our bodies need in varying quantities for survival. Major minerals, such as calcium, are required in larger amounts, while trace minerals like iron and zinc are required in smaller amounts.

calcium Vital for bone health, calcium is also important for muscle contraction and blood pressure regulation. Calcium-rich foods include low-fat milk, fish, and vegetables such as broccoli and spinach.

chromium A trace element that is important for metabolism and insulin function in the body.

copper This trace mineral is essential for proper iron processing. It is also involved in healing and metabolism.

folate Folate helps produce and maintain new cell growth and may help fight cancer.

iron This mineral helps the body transport and use oxygen, and also plays a role in immune function, temperature regulation, cognitive development, and energy metabolism.

manganese This trace mineral is needed for proper metabolism of carbohydrates, fats, and proteins. It also keeps bones and teeth healthy.

phosphorus Phosphorus helps build strong bones and teeth, and helps the body get energy from food.

potassium Potassium helps the body maintain water and mineral balance, and regulates heartbeat and blood pressure.

selenium This trace mineral works with vitamin E as an antioxidant to protect cells from damage, and also boosts immune function.

zinc Zinc promotes a healthy immune system and is critical for proper blood clotting, thyroid function, and optimal growth and reproduction.

phytochemicals

Numbering more than 10,000 known to date, these plant-based compounds have a positive effect on the body. Deeply pigmented fruits and vegetables tend to be highest in phytochemicals, but they are also found in tea, chocolate, and nuts. Familiar phytonutrient groups include carotenoids and polyphenols.

phytonutrients

Another word for phytochemicals.

polyphenols

A class of antioxidant chemicals present in deeply pigmented fruits and vegetable as well as tea, which may help protect the heart and fight cancer.

protein

Made of amino acids, protein provides the building blocks our bodies need to synthesize cells, tissues, hormones, and antibodies. It is found in foods of animal and vegetable origin, although animal proteins contain more of the amino acids our bodies need to synthesize protein. Choose lean protein sources like fish, poultry, and legumes.

sulfur compounds

Powerful substances found in cruciferous vegetables that help prevent cancer and contribute to eye health.

vitamins

Our bodies require vitamins in order to function properly. They fall into two categories: fat-soluble vitamins, which require fat for absorption and are stored in our body's fat tissue, and water-soluble vitamins, which cannot be stored and must be replenished often.

vitamin A Found in dairy products, yellow-orange fruits and vegetables, and dark green leafy vegetables, vitamin A promotes healthy skin, hair, bones, and vision. It also works as an antioxidant.

B vitamins This group of water-soluble vitamins can be found in a range of fruits and vegetables, whole grains, and dairy and meat products and includes vitamins B6 and B12, biotin, niacin, pantothenic acid, thiamin, folate, and riboflavin. Each one plays a vital role in bodily functions, including regulating metabolism and energy production, keeping the nerves and muscles healthy, and protecting against birth defects and heart disease. Choline, found in eggs, grains, and other foods, helps with brain and memory development, nutrient transport, and essential cell functions.

vitamin C This water-soluble vitamin helps build body tissues, fights infection, helps keep gums healthy, and helps the body absorb iron. It also works as an antioxidant. It can be found in many fruits and vegetables, especially citrus.

vitamin D Instrumental in building and maintaining healthy bones and teeth, vitamin D can be found in fish such as salmon and sardines, as well as in fortified milk and cereal.

vitamin E Found in nuts and seeds, whole grains, dark green vegetables, and beans, vitamin E helps form red blood cells, prevents oxidation of LDL cholesterol, and improves immunity. It also works in the body as an antioxidant.

vitamin K Necessary for protein synthesis as well as blood clotting, vitamin K can be found in dark green vegetables, asparagus, and cabbage.

basics

These staple recipes include flavorful dressings, sauces, condiments, and seasonings that will enhance a variety of dishes. Use them as part of any healthy meal.

Pico de Gallo

3 tomatoes

½ red onion

2–4 serrano chiles

1 tablespoon finely chopped
fresh cilantro

2 teaspoons fresh lime juice

Sea salt

Finely chop the tomatoes and onion into equal-size pieces. Seed and mince the chiles.

In a large bowl, stir together the tomatoes, onion, chiles, cilantro, lime juice, and 2 teaspoons salt. Let the salsa stand for 1 hour to blend the flavors.

Serve right away, or cover and store in the refrigerator for up to 3 days.

Makes about 1½ cups (12 fl oz/375 ml)

Gremolata

⅔ cup (1 oz/30 g) minced fresh
flat-leaf parsley

Finely grated zest of 1 lemon

2 cloves garlic, minced

In a small bowl, stir together the parsley, lemon zest, and garlic. Serve over cooked fish, chicken, meat, or steamed vegetables.

Makes about ¾ cup (1½ oz/45 g)

Romesco Dressing

2 tablespoons extra-virgin olive oil

1 tablespoon fresh orange juice

2 tablespoons sherry vinegar

¼ teaspoon Spanish sweet smoked paprika

2 cloves garlic, minced

3 jarred piquillo peppers, drained

1½ tablespoons chopped blanched almonds

Sea salt and freshly ground pepper

In a food processor, combine the olive oil, orange juice, vinegar, paprika, garlic, piquillo peppers, almonds,

a scant ½ teaspoon salt, and a few grindings of pepper. Process until a relatively smooth dressing forms, about 15 seconds. Taste and adjust the seasoning.

Makes about ¾ cup (6 fl oz/180 ml)

Sun-Dried Tomato Vinaigrette

4 dry-packed sun-dried tomato halves

Boiling water as needed

¼ cup (2 fl oz/60 ml) extra-virgin olive oil

3 tablespoons fresh lemon juice

1 tablespoon finely chopped fresh
flat-leaf parsley

1 tablespoon finely chopped fresh dill

1 teaspoon grated orange zest

1 small clove garlic, minced

Sea salt and freshly ground pepper

Place the sun-dried tomatoes in a heatproof bowl, pour over boiling water to cover, and let stand for 5 minutes. Drain the tomatoes and finely dice. In a small bowl, whisk together the olive oil, lemon juice, sun-dried tomatoes, parsley, dill, orange zest, garlic, 2 tablespoons water, ½ teaspoon salt, and a grinding or two of pepper until blended.

Makes about ¾ cup (6 fl oz/180 ml)

Pesto

1 tablespoon pine nuts

½ cup (4 fl oz/125 ml) extra-virgin olive oil

2 large cloves garlic

Sea salt and freshly ground pepper

1½ cups (1½ oz/45 g) tightly packed
fresh basil leaves

¼ cup (½ oz/15 g) coarsely chopped
fresh spinach leaves

2 tablespoons freshly grated
Parmesan cheese

In a dry frying pan, toast the nuts until lightly browned and fragrant, about 3 minutes; watch carefully, as they burn easily. Immediately pour onto a plate to stop the cooking and let cool.

In a food processor, combine the olive oil, pine nuts, garlic, and ½ teaspoon salt. Pulse, scraping down the sides as needed, until fairly smooth. Add the basil, spinach, and ¼ teaspoon pepper and process until blended, but still with some texture. Transfer to a glass or ceramic bowl and stir in the cheese.

Makes about 1 cup (8 fl oz/250)

Buttermilk-Herb Sauce

$1/3$ cup ($1/2$ oz/15 g) lightly packed, coarsely chopped fresh flat-leaf parsley

2 tablespoons lightly packed, coarsely chopped fresh dill

1 tablespoon coarsely chopped fresh mint

1 green onion, including tender green tops, thinly sliced

$1/2$ cup (4 fl oz/125 ml) low-fat buttermilk

$1/2$ cup (4 fl oz/125 g) nonfat plain yogurt

1 tablespoon extra-virgin olive oil

Sea salt

In a food processor, combine the parsley, dill, mint, and green onion and process until finely chopped. Add the buttermilk, yogurt, olive oil, and $1/2$ teaspoon salt and process until the ingredients are blended.

Pour the dressing into a container with a tight-fitting lid and refrigerate for several hours or overnight before serving; it will thicken.

Shake or stir well before serving over green salads, tomatoes, steamed vegetables, chicken, or fish. It will keep in the refrigerator for up to 3 days.

Makes $1^{1}/4$ cups (10 fl oz/310 ml)

Roasted Tomato Sauce

7 ripe plum tomatoes, cored

2–3 serrano chiles, seeded and minced

$1/2$ small onion, chopped

1 large clove garlic, chopped

1 tablespoon canola or grapeseed oil

Sea salt

In a dry frying pan over high heat, roast the tomatoes, turning them as they char slightly, about 5 minutes.

In a food processor, combine the tomatoes, chiles, onion, and garlic. Process until blended but still chunky.

In a large frying pan over medium-high heat, warm the oil. Add the tomato mixture and cook, stirring constantly, until thickened, about 5 minutes. Taste and adjust the seasoning.

Makes about $1^{1}/2$ cups (12 fl oz/375 ml)

Sweetened Whipped Cream

$1/2$ cup (4 fl oz/125 ml) cold heavy cream

2 teaspoons sugar

$1/2$ teaspoon pure vanilla extract

In a chilled bowl, combine the heavy cream, sugar, and vanilla. Using a whisk, beat until soft peaks form. (Alternatively, using an electric mixer, beat on medium-high speed until soft peaks form.)

Use the cream right away, or cover and refrigerate until serving time.

Makes about 1 cup (8 fl oz/250 ml)

Fruit Sauce

2 cups (8 oz/250 g) raspberries, strawberries, blueberries, or mango cubes

$2^{1}/2$ tablespoons honey

$1^{1}/2$ teaspoons fresh lemon juice

In a food processor, combine the fruit and honey and pulse just until puréed. Pour the purée through a fine-mesh sieve set over a bowl, pressing on the purée with the back of a wooden spoon to remove any seeds. Stir in the lemon juice. Cover and refrigerate for up to 5 days. Serve over pancakes, waffles, angel food cake, fresh fruit, or yogurt.

Makes about 2 cups (16 fl oz/500 ml)

Homemade Yogurt

1 qt (1 l) nonfat milk

$1/3$ cup instant nonfat dried milk

2 tablespoons plain nonfat yogurt (make sure it contains live, active cultures and is made without gelatin or stabilizers)

In a large, heavy saucepan, bring the milk just to a boil, stirring to prevent a skin from forming. If a skin does form, skim it off with a spoon. Remove from the heat and let cool to 112°–115°F (44°–46°C).

Put the dried milk in a clean ceramic or glass bowl. Gradually whisk in about $1/2$ cup of the warm milk until the mixture is smooth. Whisk in the yogurt until well blended. Slowly whisk in the remaining warm milk until blended.

Cover the dish tightly with plastic wrap and set in a warm place (90°-100°F/35°–38°C) without moving or disturbing the bowl, until thickened to your liking, 6–8 hours or overnight. (An oven with a gas pilot light is a good choice; if you have an electric oven, preheat it to 120°F/49°C, then turn it off. The longer the yogurt stands, the tarter and thicker it will become.

Use the yogurt right away, or refrigerate it for up to 4 days.

Makes about 2 cups (16 fl oz/500 ml)

index

weldon**owen**

415 Jackson Street, Suite 200, San Francisco, CA 94111
www.weldonowen.com

GOOD FOR YOU

Conceived and produced by Weldon Owen, Inc.
In collaboration with Williams-Sonoma, Inc.
3250 Van Ness Avenue, San Francisco, CA 94109

A WELDON OWEN PRODUCTION

Copyright © 2013 Weldon Owen, Inc.
and Williams-Sonoma, Inc.
All rights reserved, including the right of reproduction
in whole or in part in any form.

Printed and bound in China

First printed in 2012
10 9 8 7 6 5 4 3

Library of Congress Control Number: 2012949839

ISBN 13: 978-1-61628-494-7
ISBN 10: 1-61628-494-3

Weldon Owen is a division of
BONNIER

WELDON OWEN, INC.

CEO and President Terry Newell
VP, Sales and Marketing Amy Kaneko
Director of Finance Mark Perrigo

VP and Publisher Hannah Rahill
Executive Editor Jennifer Newens

Creative Director Emma Boys
Art Director Ali Zeigler
Designer Rachel Lopez Metzger
Production Director Chris Hemesath
Production Manager Michelle Duggan

Photographer Erin Kunkel
Food Stylist Valerie Aikman-Smith
Prop Stylist Christine Wolheim

ACKNOWLEDGMENTS

Weldon Owen wishes to thank the following people for their generous support
in producing this book: David Bornfriend, Kim Laidlaw, Ashley Lima,
Eve Lynch, Elizabeth Parson, Jason Wheeler